"Becoming a gardener is challenging, but Nicole Burke is a trustworthy, encouraging teacher. She breaks down intimidating methods into step-by-step instructions with easy-to-follow advice, so you can confidently build and cultivate a beautiful kitchen garden in your own backyard."
—Grace Haynes, *Southern Living Magazine*

"An absolutely delightful read! Everything you'll ever need for creating your own kitchen garden including motivation and inspiration. Nicole makes gardening approachable and fun no matter what color your thumbs are."
-Myquillyn Smith, *Wall Street Journal* Best Selling author of *Cozy Minimalist Home*

"In this beautifully executed book, Nicole takes us by the hand and walks us down the garden path—showing us step-by-step how we can start growing our own food in simple, sensible, and stylish ways. If you're brand new to kitchen gardening, this book is a great primer; and if you're an old pro, the garden designs she has laid out in relation to the home, will inspire you to rethink your own foodscape."
—Summer Rayne Oakes, author of *How to Make a Plant Love You: Cultivate Green Space in Your Home and Heart*

"Whether you are starting a vegetable garden for the first time or are troubleshooting the garden you already have, *Kitchen Garden Revival* is required reading. Not only is it packed with important information, Nicole's warm and tender voice guides you through each step of the growing process with encouragement and wisdom."
—Lauri Kranz, author of *A Garden Can Be Anywhere* and Owner of Edible Gardens LA

"Nicole's passion for kitchen gardening is inspiring yet also realistic. I can now see the potential for my own dingy yard to become a garden that fits my busy lifestyle and nourishes my family."
—Jen Hansard, author of the Best Selling Book *Simple Green Smoothies*

"Instead of talking about the many social, emotional, and environmental problems of our time, *Kitchen Garden Revival* offers a simple, practical way to do our part in mitigating stress, anxiety, depression, food waste, plastic pollution, and climate change—all by starting your very own kitchen garden. Since starting my own kitchen garden, I've had hundreds of people ask me for resources for starting their own gardens, and I'm excited to finally have an answer for them. *Kitchen Garden Revival* is a complete, detailed, and straightforward guide to planning, installing, tending, and harvesting an aesthetically pleasing and productive garden and, best of all, it's accessible to everyone, including the person who has never grown a seed, knows nothing about soil, and can't imagine what to plant where and when. I think what I like best is that Nicole doesn't mince words—she's straightforward and to the point, and offers a truly can-do approach to realizing the kitchen garden of your dreams."
—Julia Watkins, author of *Simply Living Well*

"Nicole Burke's *Kitchen Garden Revival* is certain to inspire home cooks and professional chefs alike. I was first introduced to container gardening by my best friend and mentor P. Allen Smith. As a chef, container gardening and raised beds have found their place in my kitchen gardens at my historic home and my restaurant. This book will not only create a revival of kitchen gardens but there will be a whole lot of Hallelujahs and Amens when you're done!"
—Regina Charboneau, chef, restauranteur, cookbook author

"*Kitchen Garden Revival* is just the book I've been looking for! A fun read that makes gardening approachable, accessible and enjoyable—without overcomplicating it. With a clean layout, loads of beautiful pictures, and a relatable voice, Nicole Burke will inspire anyone interested in gardening to get outside and get their hands dirty, reminding us all that growing food is something we should be celebrating together."
—Timothy Pakron, author of *Mississippi Vegan*

KITCHEN GARDEN REVIVAL

A Modern Guide to Creating a Stylish Small-Scale,
Low-Maintenance Edible Garden

Nicole Johnsey Burke

Photography by Eric Kelley

COOL
SPRINGS
PRESS

Quarto.com

© 2020 Quarto Publishing Group USA Inc.
Text © 2020 Nicole Burke

First Published in 2020 by Cool Springs Press, an imprint of The Quarto Group,
100 Cummings Center, Suite 265-D, Beverly, MA 01915, USA.
T (978) 282-9590 F (978) 283-2742

Cool Springs Press titles are also available at discount for retail, wholesale, promotional, and bulk purchase. For details, contact the Special Sales Manager by email at specialsales@quarto.com or by mail at The Quarto Group, Attn: Special Sales Manager, 100 Cummings Center, Suite 265-D, Beverly, MA 01915, USA.

24   11

ISBN: 978-0-7603-6686-8

Digital edition published in 2020
eISBN: 978-0-7603-6687-5

Library of Congress Cataloging-in-Publication Data available

Design: Laura Klynstra
Cover Image: Eric Kelley
Photography: Eric Kelley

Printed in China

FOR JASON,

who built our first kitchen garden.

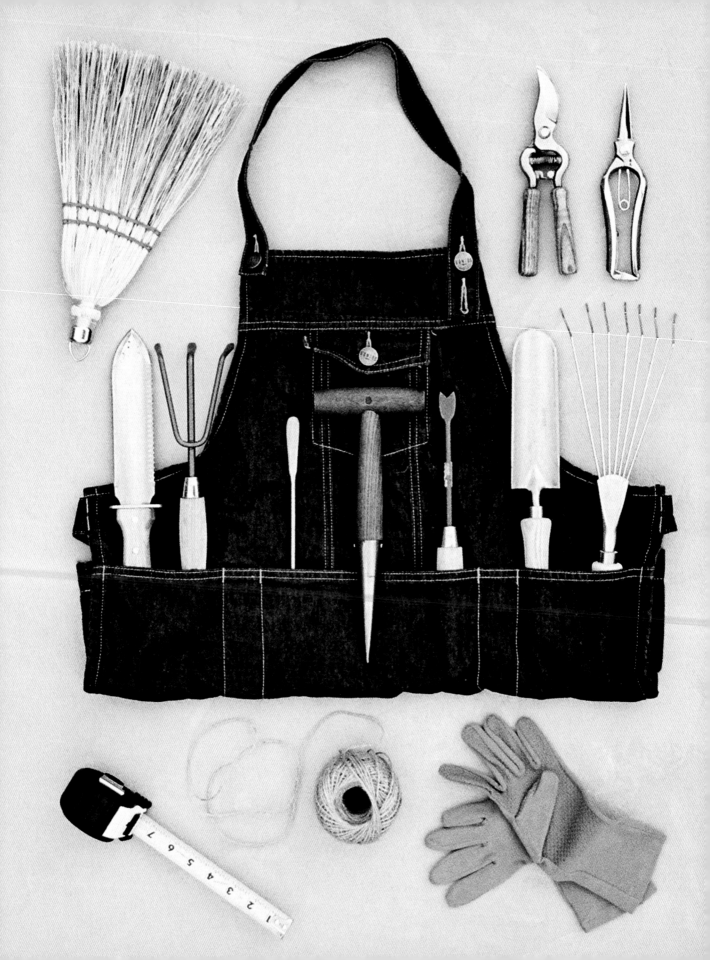

CONTENTS

PREFACE

● ● ● ● ● ●

A few things will happen before you finish reading this book.

First, if you don't already, you'll start calling yourself a "gardener." It might seem awkward at first (I've been there) but, go ahead, take a moment, look in the mirror, and say these words out loud: *I am a gardener*. From now on, when you introduce yourself to others, type out your bio or profile, you'll include "gardener" in your list of attributes. Deal?

Though this may not yet be the case, gardening is soon to become part of you, part of your identity, and definitely part of your whole and happy lifestyle. It will be a skill you're proud of, a hobby you enjoy, a gift you share with neighbors, friends, and family.

Beyond calling yourself a "gardener," you'll soon refer to a specific spot on your property as the "kitchen garden." You've got the patio, the front porch, maybe the lawn and the driveway. So, now, let's put "kitchen garden" on the map, too. You're about to have a new special place, a getaway, an escape from reality. But good news: it's right outside your back door.

You're not just going to have a new bio and a new happy place, you'll also gain a bigger appreciation for the place you call home. The unique aspects of your community, your seasons, and your weather will give you a greater appreciation for what your little plot of Earth can do. You'll discover the foods that grow perfectly where you live—and those that just won't. You'll see how your seasons are distinct and different. And all these things will make your town, your city, your community not just a place where you live, but a spot on Earth you belong to. As someone who's moved a lot, I know this as fact: It feels really good to belong somewhere.

And beyond appreciating your particular plot, you'll soon start thinking of food as a wonder: nothing short of supernatural. Not something to avoid, not a calorie to count. After you watch a tiny seed become a huge basket full of delicious salad or a little plant become a giant bowl of soup, you won't be able to un-see it. And you won't want to. A carrot is about to become a unicorn to you, and it's the very best feeling.

Lastly, this book will help you see that you're a change-maker, part of something bigger, someone doing real good in the world. From now on, when you hear talk of global warming or icecaps melting or food miles, when the news talks about local economic challenges or lack of natural resources, you'll know you're doing your part to help and learning to do more. You've got a tangible, doable plan right in front of you to start making change today.

How can I promise so much from one little gardening book?

I'm just recounting my story, the stories of the hundreds of clients I've served through Rooted Garden, and the thousands of people I've taught online through Gardenary.

It was just a few years ago when I felt like a total fake calling myself a "gardener" (I'd killed my fair share of plants). As a woman who's struggled with an eating disorder, I've seen food as something to avoid or use in an unhealthy way. Married to a smart scientist obtaining degrees and experience, I've moved more than five times in the last fifteen years and wondered how in the world each new place could ever feel like "home." And, even though it's important to me, I, too, still wonder if I'm making any real, good difference in this world. But, it's not an exaggeration for me to say, having my kitchen garden has been part of the answer to almost all of it.

And I know it will be for you, too.

So, now that you know how this story will end, let's begin.

A DEFINITION

kitchen garden   a garden where vegetables, fruits, and herbs are grown for everyday use in the kitchen

INTRODUCTION

What's a Kitchen Garden and Why It's Time for a Revival

• • • • •

"So, what exactly is a kitchen garden? Is it a garden inside the kitchen?" (I get this question a lot).

Called kailyards in Scotland and known as potagers in France (sounds fancy, right?), a kitchen garden is a place closely connected with your kitchen and everyday life. It's a distinct area of your home and landscape where vegetables, fruits, and herbs are grown for culinary use.

A kitchen garden can be as small as a collection of garden boxes on the patio or deck or it can be as large as a formal stone garden that covers hundreds of square feet. No matter the size, the purpose is the same: a garden that's tended regularly and used frequently in everyday meals.

It's not a vegetable patch or homestead. It's much smaller and doesn't require nearly the amount of work those do. Unlike a farm, which is cleared all at once, planted all at once, and harvested (you guessed it) all at once, a kitchen garden is tended regularly. And different from row cropping or a big vegetable patch, a kitchen garden is a space for growing either a small sample of a wide variety of plants or a large amount of a small variety of plants. In other words, you're not going to avoid the grocery store entirely, but you will skip past certain items (which is a very good feeling, by the way).

Instead of a rambling field or an entire yard planted with vegetables, a kitchen garden is separate from the rest of the landscape and created to be a central feature. It's not something to tuck behind the garage and hide from neighbors. It's set up to be beautiful—front and center. It's a special centerpiece of your home life, a place to entertain and have guests, or just hang out with family.

At the very least, kitchen gardens can provide all the herbs you'll need year-round (either cut fresh or dried and stored). Beyond that, kitchen gardens can yield most of the greens you and your family eat. And greater still, kitchen gardens can provide large amounts of beans, peppers, squash, cucumbers, and other fresh vegetables in the height of their season as well as opportunity for preserved foods for even the coldest winters.

The dictionary has its own definition of "kitchen garden" but after years of working in my garden and with hundreds of clients and students, here's mine: a kitchen garden is the missing piece in the pursuit of a whole and happy life.

Why Kitchen Garden?

Mental health is quickly becoming the key indicator of overall well-being. Depression, anxiety, stress, and burnout are all serious in themselves, but those challenges are also linked to cancer, high blood pressure, and heart disease. Our minds and bodies are connected in ways we're just starting to understand, and, in this fast-paced and demanding world, we've got to find ways to slow down, reconnect with nature, and care for ourselves again.

For Yourself

When you learn to grow yourself you literally grow your self. The biggest reason to have a kitchen garden is for your happiness. Stepping outside into the garden each day has been proven to help do just that. And there's no more practical way to push you outside than if the tastiest parts of dinner are growing inside that garden.

You have to eat anyway, so why not pursue a mindful activity that not only feeds your mind and soul but also fills your stomach?

A kitchen garden may just be the most practical hobby you can pursue. You'll learn new skills, get exercise, wake up your senses each time you step outdoors, and return with an armload of fresh food.

For Your Community

Over the last few decades, there's been a growing interest in knowing our foods' sources, returning to organic growing methods, and appreciating the nutrients available when eating freshly picked food. The kitchen garden is a key part of the this movement. Although the garden won't provide the entirety of your family's fruit and vegetable needs, it gives you a taste of what's growing locally, an appreciation for the process of growing organic and natural food, and a connection to the growers and farmers in your area. Nearly all my clients with a kitchen garden often also have a Community Supported Agriculture (CSA) membership to supplement their gardens. Once they taste a freshly harvested carrot or a tomato just picked from the vine, they can't return to the shipped stuff at the grocery store.

By eating locally you'll be more connected to your local community—better understanding your particular seasons, appreciating the unique foods you can grow in your area, and supporting people doing great work there.

For the World

No matter your position on global warming, we likely all agree things aren't changing for the better. And although it's not the only contributor, a few major aspects of our Earth's trouble are food miles, packaging, and waste. Currently, most of the food consumed in America has traveled more than 1,500 miles (2,400 km) before reaching the consumers' plate. The petroleum demand on food is huge. By growing food in your personal kitchen garden and eating locally from farmers and CSAs, you vastly reduce the number of miles your food needs to travel.

Beyond the miles, food that's shipped across the country, or internationally, is also heavily packaged. Our plastic consumption in North America is at an all-time high and a lot of that is due to the enormous amount of plastic used to package our shipped food. The kitchen garden is one part of the answer to this issue. Even if you just grow greens and herbs in your kitchen garden, you'll make a serious cut in your plastic waste in just a few months.

Why a Kitchen Garden Revival?

Kitchen gardens, though we may have forgotten the term, aren't a new concept. They've been a thing for thousands of years.

But somewhere along our way of progress, we lost the kitchen garden. With the input of technology and industry, our food systems have changed dramatically over the last century. And while not all the change has been bad, the kitchen garden is something that should've stayed. To create whole and happy lives, for the beauty in our homes, for the benefit of our community and for the good of the world, it's time for a kitchen garden revival.

A revival is a magical thing. It's something I can wish for but not really something I (or any one person) can make happen alone. It's like a seed that starts small and is barely noticeable at first. It must be buried and grow strong roots (even when no one notices). There are 1,000 things that could go wrong, but with just the right amount of rain and sunshine, and not too many weeds or pests, that seed can grow so big and so fast that no one could tell where the vine begins or ends.

Perhaps this book will be that seed. (Fingers crossed!) But I'll need *you* to bring the rain and the sunshine.

You can begin with just a pot of garlic chives on the front porch. Or, build a formal *potager*. Wherever you are, there's a kitchen garden that fits. And if you have a kitchen (and I'm sure you do), you need a kitchen garden.

By picking up this book, you're already part of the *Kitchen Garden Revival*. Your interest to read this far means you're a part of the vine that's growing from that tiny seed. And I can't wait to see how big you, your garden, and this movement will grow.

Before you begin, go to www.gardenary.com/book and download your free Gardenary Journal. The Gardenary Journal will guide you through every step of setting up, planting, and harvesting from your kitchen garden.

Thank you in advance for bringing back the kitchen garden with me. Now, let's go plant some seeds together.

Download your free Gardenary Journal or find a garden coach to help guide you through this book at www.gardenary.com/book.

CHAPTER ONE

SITE

Find the Perfect Kitchen Garden Spot

· · · · ·

Picture a place that's special to you—a spot you head to take a break, enjoy yourself, discover something new, spend time with people you love, or just reconnect with nature.

Now tell me: Did you picture a place far away or one nearby? Were you home or did you skip town? And, if you had to leave town (and most people do), do you think it's possible to create a space that could be all those things but, instead, is right outside your back door?

Imagination, meet kitchen garden, a retreat and a getaway waiting for you in the backyard, on the porch, or just along the fence, your new escape from reality even when reality is just a few steps away.

In this chapter, you'll face the challenging task of picking the site for your kitchen garden.

Choosing your kitchen garden's location can be a tough decision. It's one of the key tasks our garden coaches at Gardenary and my team at Rooted Garden do every day: we help clients make the choice between the left side of the backyard, the spot along the driveway, or the space next to the patio.

Choosing the location for your garden is tough for good reason—location means everything. In some cases, the decision may have already been made for you if you have only limited space, just a patio, or only one patch of ground that gets sunlight. And, for others, you may have countless spaces where a garden could belong. In both scenarios, there's more to the decision than you think.

Let's start with a message for the perfectionists and overachievers: there's no such thing as a perfect location. At least, it's very rare that you'll find it, especially if you live in the city.

But even without a perfect spot, delicious food will grow beautifully in the space you have available. Something edible, possibly dozens of edible choices, will thrive in your space. There's always room for you to grow your self.

Key Site Considerations

Picking the best spot for your kitchen garden isn't just about opinion or the flip of a coin. It's about balancing priorities and considerations. After designing hundreds of gardens, I've created a system that works to help you sort through the options.

There are four key aspects to consider before choosing your kitchen garden site:

1. Sunlight exposure

2. Water proximity

3. Convenience

4. Aesthetics

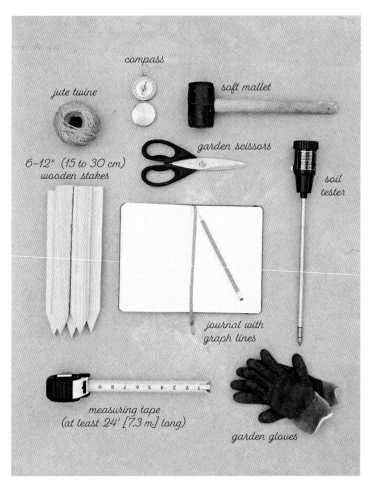

compass

jute twine

soft mallet

6–12" (15 to 30 cm) wooden stakes

garden scissors

soil tester

journal with graph lines

measuring tape (at least 24' [7.3 m] long)

garden gloves

(Nearly) PERFECT KITCHEN GARDEN LOCATION

» 6 or more direct sunlight hours per day, all year

» Proximity to a water source

» Near the kitchen and common household traffic

» Ties in aesthetically to the existing landscape

» Large enough space for your desired garden size and shape

My very scientific calculation has determined that exactly 60 percent of this decision should be based on sunlight; 20 percent on water accessibility; and the final 20 percent of the decision is split between convenience and aesthetics.

It's true. I did say there's no such thing as a perfect spot for the kitchen garden, but there is a perfect formula. As you select your garden location, the goal is to find a location that matches this blueprint as closely as possible: receives six or more hours of sunlight per day, is near a water source, and is located as close to the kitchen and your everyday activities as possible. You also want a spot that will tie in well to the rest of your landscape and is able to accommodate the size necessary to hold the amount of vegetables and fruit you'd like to harvest.

Each of these aspects should be considered, as they all matter. But some matter more. At least 60 percent of your decision should be based on the available sunlight. So, we'll start there and then consider the other three aspects.

To look at each aspect of the formula, let's create a map of your property. You may just have a balcony and that's fine. Still, make a map. To start, draw your home and yard to scale on a piece of graph paper (there's a spot to do this inside the downloadable Gardenary Journal you'll find at gardenary.com/book).

Once you've drawn your home and yard to scale, draw a compass to denote the cardinal directions as they relate to your home and yard. Now that you've determined where North and South are located, let's find the sunshine.

This is the spot I chose to place my kitchen garden because it receives the most amount of sunlight of any spot in my yard, it's near a water spigot, close to my kitchen window, and works well with the front yard aesthetics of my modern farmhouse home.

MAP YOUR SITE

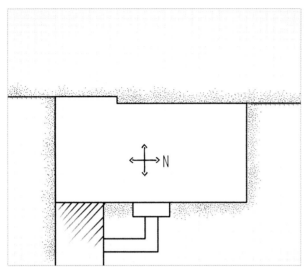

1. Draw your home and yard to scale. Find the cardinal directions and mark them on the map

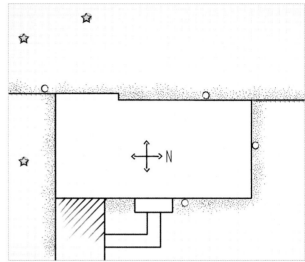

2. Add stars to the spots that receive the most sunlight and circles to note spigot locations.

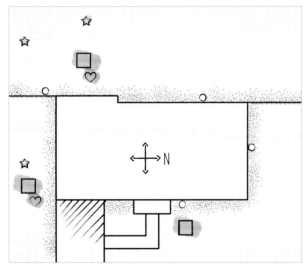

3. Add squares to note accessible spots and hearts to note spots where the garden would be most pleasing to the eye.

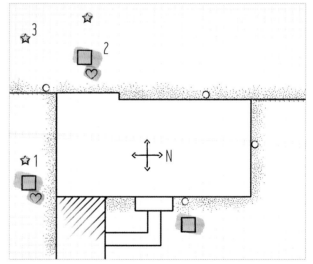

4. Consider all the aspects and number your kitchen garden locations in order of preference.

This garden is on the southern side of the fence and far from the home for midday and afternoon sun.

This garden is on the southern side of the home, with limited morning and evening sunshine but lots of midday sun.

This garden is on the southern side of the fence and receives midday and afternoon sun.

This garden is on the southern side of the home. The home blocks morning light but the garden location receives sunlight from midday until the end of the day.

Sunlight

As much sunlight on your kitchen garden as possible—that's the goal. Sounds simple, right? But getting hours and hours of light on your garden throughout the year is difficult, especially if you live in the city.

Even if you do see lots of sunlight in a certain spot during part of the year, it may only be like that for one season. In our Houston home, we watched a plot in our yard receive more than eight hours of sun all summer long. So, as soon as autumn arrived, we planted our kitchen garden right in that very spot. I'm not kidding when I tell you that, the very day we filled the beds with soil, I walked outside to see nothing but shadows on our new kitchen garden.

The challenge was that our garden was on the north side of our fence and on the other side of that fence was a giant oak tree. During the middle of summer when the sun was at its height in the sky, this wasn't an issue. But, as soon as our Northern Hemisphere began to tilt away from the sun, that oak tree and fence were suddenly standing right between the sunlight and our garden's promise of autumn carrots and winter peas. Bummer.

Though it may seem that the sun is directly overhead most of the day, the truth is, it's always shining on us from an angle. In the Northern Hemisphere, the sun is shining on us from the south, and in the Southern Hemisphere, it's the opposite. It's during the winter months that you'll realize this is the case. On the longest day of the year, the sun is nearly straight overhead but, on the shortest day of the year, it can be quite low on the horizon, depending on your longitude. And if there's a tall structure standing between your garden and the sun's leaning, your garden may only see a shadow for nearly half the year.

To avoid these shadows, place your garden on the other side of any tall structure that would stand between your garden and the winter sunshine. In other words, if you're in the Northern Hemisphere, place the garden on the southern side of tall structures such as your home, a tree line, or fences. If you're in the Southern Hemisphere, place it on the north side.

No matter what side you're on, the truth is that most of us live in cities and tight quarters and, sometimes, the most light our garden can receive is significantly less than six hours.

If this is the case for you, don't stop reading. There are loads of edible plants that will grow in just a few hours of sunlight. In part 2, you'll learn how to plan your plants based on your sunlight hours.

If the spot you've selected, or have available, receives less than four hours of sunlight per day in any season, you'll need to prioritize growing greens in

PLANT/HOURS *of* SUNLIGHT REQUIRED

Beans, Peas, Root Crops: 6 hours per day

Greens: 2 to 4 hours per day

Herbs: 4+ hours per day

Tomatoes, Peppers: 8+ hours per day

that spot, such as herbs and lettuces. If it receives four to six hours of sun per day, you can grow root vegetables, and if it receives more than six hours of sunlight per day, you can grow leaves, roots, and plenty of fruit.

Our garden that ended up in full shade in autumn and winter was perfect for growing loads of greens, and I mean *loads*. The root crops and peas did eventually produce; they just took twice as long to do so.

After marking the cardinal directions on your map, place a star in each spot of the yard that receives maximum sunlight throughout the year. Congratulations! You've just narrowed your location choices. Now, let's consider the second matter: water.

Water Source

After sunlight, the second item to prioritize for your kitchen garden is its proximity to a water source. Consistent water is key to your success. Nature's water is best but also unpredictable. And most vegetables and fruiting plants thrive with water schedules they can rely upon. For this reason, think about the available water supply before choosing the site for your kitchen garden.

If you're installing your gardens during a rainy season or in early spring when the weather seems cool and moist, a water source may be a complete afterthought. Even if it isn't, you might just be so excited about your garden that you're picturing yourself with your watering can, walking from plant to plant each morning before sunrise.

Trust me: your excitement won't last forever. The watering chore, nostalgic as it sounds, will feel like the chore that it is fairly quickly. And nothing about wilting or dead plants (waiting for you to show up with your watering can) feels nostalgic.

If possible, place your garden near a spigot, a rain barrel, or where it can easily connect to a formal irrigation system. If using a spigot, be certain you can attach either a hose or drip system from the water source to the garden area. If using a rain barrel, ensure that water can run from the barrel to the garden beds. And, finally, if you have a formal irrigation system in place, situate the garden in such a way that the lines can be brought into your garden bed with as little digging and repositioning as necessary (more on water connection in chapter 4).

Before moving on, mark all the spigots, rain barrels, or irrigation hookups in your home or yard on your garden map with a circle.

Convenience

The third consideration for your kitchen garden space is the convenience of each potential area. When we meet with Rooted Garden and Gardenary clients, some want their kitchen garden hidden from the home—just in case it gets unruly. This is actually the way to ensure that very thing happens. Out of sight, out of mind isn't just a saying. It's a thing.

Because it is a kitchen garden, it makes sense to have it as close to your kitchen as possible, right?

Picture yourself prepping dinner and just starting to serve soup when you think: Fresh chives on top would be just the thing. How close should the garden be for you to walk out with your scissors?

Or, imagine prepping a salad jar for your work lunch early in the morning. How far are you willing to walk to cut some lettuce before packing up?

If you can keep the garden as close to the kitchen as possible, you'll use it and tend it more frequently.

My first successful kitchen garden was right alongside the driveway. As a busy working mom, I was able to check up on the garden just by driving into the garage. Even if I only had a second, I could quickly see if things were wilting, notice holes on the leaves, or note when things were ready to harvest (yay!). I'm fairly certain this proximity to our daily activities made all the difference in my kitchen garden success, and I'm sure it will do the same for you.

So, mark the most accessible spots in your landscape with a square.

Aesthetic

Ever felt a little awkward? (Raises hand). Between wrangling four kids, dirt under my fingernails, and lots of moving, I tend to keep finding ways not to fit in. Although I'm okay with standing out as a person, "awkward" is just not the look we're going for with the kitchen garden. Instead, the goal is to "fit in" with the rest of the landscape. Don't get me wrong: The kitchen garden should (and will) stand out because of its beauty but we don't want it to draw attention just because it doesn't fit in with the rest of the landscape.

Here's how to avoid that situation.

First, look for natural spots where a garden could fit. Possible spots include a side yard, along a fence, or as an extension of an existing structure, such as a deck or patio. Look for ways to connect your kitchen garden to the rest of the landscape by lining up or being near existing structures or plantings.

Second, look for areas where your garden could match some measurements of other pieces of your landscape. If the deck is a certain height, design the beds to measure the same. If the building comes out to a certain width, design the beds to come out to that width as well. By selecting existing elements in your landscape to match to the garden, you'll give your garden a sense of belonging.

Opposite: A Rooted Garden client's garden is just outside her kitchen door, making it easy to harvest herbs and greens as a meal is being prepared.

This formal potager starts at the edge of the porch and connects with the lines of the home, making it look more like it belongs and has been there from the beginning.

As you design your layout in the next section be sure to group elements within the kitchen garden. Don't just throw a box out there by itself. If the kitchen garden is going to stand out, be sure it has friends to stand alongside it. If you're just creating one box, add fruit trees, a birdbath, potted herbs, or something else to group alongside the garden.

Keep these three principles in mind and save your kitchen garden from that "one of these things is not like the other" scenario. Place a heart on the spaces on your map where a kitchen garden would fit well with the landscape or continue a line or design from your home or other existing structures.

Now it's time to weigh all four considerations and select the top garden site choices. Keep each aspect in mind, sunlight being most important, water being essential, and then convenience and aesthetics. Choose your top three to four locations (if there are that many possibilities) and number each on the map.

Size

Now, it's time to grab a measuring tape and determine how much growing space is available in each area. Measure the width and length of each potential garden space and mark them in your journal.

This Corten steel garden was designed to match both the height and the material of the family's existing fire pit. With both measuring 18 inches (45.7 cm) the elements complement one another.

Before you plan for a huge or compact garden, consider both your input and output goals for the space. Essentially, it's time to figure out how much you have to give your garden and how much you'd like your garden to give you. Your garden size is limited by space, time, and money and can be altered to fit your output desires. Once you've decided on these constraints, you can begin to determine the best size and shape for your kitchen garden.

Input

Now that you know the total space available for each potential spot in your landscape, consider the amount of time you'll have for your garden. For time, you may have only a few minutes at the start or end of the day. Or, you may have a few hours each weekend. Adding kitchen garden duties will slowly become part of your daily routine but, if you work full-time, have kids' soccer games every weekend, or travel a lot, it's important to think about time (and time constraints) at this point, rather than after you've installed a large garden.

Time needs for the garden will vary from week to week and season to season and some plants require much less tending and attention than others, but these are the general guidelines to consider.

You'll need more time for the garden at the beginning and end of each season. In the beginning, you'll need time to find and source plants and seeds and then have an extended period of time for planting and seeding. And, at the end of each season, you'll need time to harvest and use your plants and then time to pull spent plants and start again for the following season.

In the middle of each season, you'll mostly need time to tend and regularly harvest from your garden. This can be a little each day but should come to about one minute per square foot (0.09 m²), or 30 minutes per 30-square-foot (2.78 m²) garden per week.

Basically, you need about 2 minutes per square foot (0.09 m²) for the planting and harvesting phases of the season and about 1 minute per square foot (0.09 m²) per week during the tending season.

After you consider your time, it's time to consider money. If you've spent any time online, you've likely seen all the claims that gardening will save you loads of money.

Never buy an avocado again.

Do this and you'll never spend money on celery.

Save hundreds at the grocery store each month by doing this.

These posts remind me of the time we installed our kitchen garden in Houston. My husband bought the untreated cedar and built the beds himself. We ordered the best soil we could find and we did all the shoveling. We used pine straw for the ground cover and planted nearly everything by seed. Though we did the work ourselves and tried to buy the least expensive versions of high-quality materials, we still spent more than $2,500 on our 120-square-foot (11.1 m²) kitchen garden.

I felt more than a little guilt over the cost of the whole setup, so I'd proudly report to Jason every time I skipped buying boxes of organic lettuce, kale, and parsley. "I saved $19 today!" He'd just laugh. How many grocery store trips skipping past salad boxes would it take to make up our $2,500 investment? I'll tell you the answer: too many.

There are times when harvests will save you at the grocery store. But, I'm sorry to say, the kitchen garden isn't really a way to save money, especially in the beginning. So, do yourself (and your partner) a favor and don't expect to make money on the deal.

Instead, see your garden as an investment in your home and landscape, like buying a nice piece of furniture, splurging on a beautiful piece of art, or adding on a new room.

Consider money spent in the garden like money spent on gym equipment, a club membership, or music lessons. Or, simply consider it as paying for a doctor's visit. The saying is a little lame, but it doesn't mean it's not true: "Gardening is cheaper than therapy and you get tomatoes." It would take quite a few therapy sessions to equal the cost of a kitchen garden, but you will, at least, get to eat your results.

As you plan your garden, the investment and costs will add up quickly. So, do a check on your bank account, on your home improvement budget, on your "fun money" and see how much you can afford to invest in your garden for this first round. You can start simply for a few hundred dollars or invest more significantly with a few thousand.

For money, you'll need anywhere from $25 to $50 per square foot (0.09 m²) for a DIY wood garden installation. If you'd like a kitchen garden company to install it for you, find one in your area at gardenary.com. Turnkey installation will start at around $100 per square foot (0.09 m²).

INPUT

Space in Square Feet [m²]	Average Time per Week [1½ minutes per square foot [0.09 m²]	DIY Money [$35 per square foot [0.09 m²]]	Turnkey [$100 per square foot [0.09 m²]]
25 (2.3 m²)	40 minutes	$875	$2,500
50 (4.64 m²)	75 minutes	$1,750	$5,000
75 (6.9 m²)	115 minutes	$2,625	$7,500
100 (9.29 m²)	150 minutes	$3,500	$10,000
125 (11.6 m²)	190 min	$4,375	$12,500

Estimates are for most US cities as of 2020

Output

For output, you'll get an average of about one to two harvests a month from every square foot (0.09 m²) in the garden. This is just an estimate but if you're growing in 30 square feet (2.8 m²) of garden space, you can harvest two servings of greens a day or one serving of a larger vegetable or fruit a day for about a month or two, thirty to forty days after planting.

Garden Layout

Finding the right layout for your kitchen garden is like jumping into the dressing room at your favorite store. It's exciting and intimidating at the same time. Will anything fit?

It's funny. For clients, I can almost immediately decide on the best fit and layout for their new kitchen garden. But, in my landscape, I spend a few months in the garden "dressing room," trying on one layout after another. Making decisions all by yourself can be a little tough.

When I began Rooted Garden, my limited experience led me to believe that a kitchen garden was just a wooden box placed in the middle of the yard. It seemed that one size had to fit all.

But, as I soon discovered, there's not just one, but there are dozens of ways to lay out your kitchen garden space. Before you select yours, keep these designs in mind.

Here, you'll find five of our most classic and tested designs.

Border Garden

The border garden has become our most popular layout. I think, mostly, because it fits naturally into so many spaces and often makes the most of areas of the yard that were previously underutilized. A border garden layout works well if you're limited in space, or you'd like to preserve most of your lawn or landscape for other uses. We've designed border gardens along the house, in side yards, along fences and driveways, and along the backyard's perimeter.

You'll need a minimum of 2 feet (0.6 m) of width and at least 6 feet (1.8 m) in length available to make the most of a kitchen garden in the border layout.

Border gardens are generally 1½ to 2½ feet (0.5 to 0.8 m) wide. Three sides of the garden are accessible but the other will be against your home or a fence or other structure that will block access. So, 2½ feet (0.8 m) is about the maximum width to consider.

This side yard garden makes the most of a small space with herbs growing along the wall that receives less sun and fruiting plants growing along the beds that receive more sunlight.

Installed as part of new home construction, this border garden is designed to maximize growing space while maintaining a large area of the yard for future outdoor seating.

These border gardens along the fence line make the most of this patio backyard, maintaining plenty of seating and entertaining space with herbs and greens growing in nearly all the corners.

Twin Gardens

If you've got space and can dedicate some of your central lawn to a kitchen garden, twin gardens can be a perfect match. Twin gardens allow you to grow a wider variety of plants and the design works well in the landscape. Generally, I've found that if you're not going to have a border garden, you'd rarely want one garden all by itself in the middle of the yard, so I almost always choose a minimum of two gardens unless the landscape just doesn't allow it.

Twin gardens provide a symmetrical layout that makes the most of a yard that's deeper than it is wide (or wider than it is deep). Twin gardens also allow you to maximize the growing space inside this larger garden area while creating more interest and appeal than a single garden provides.

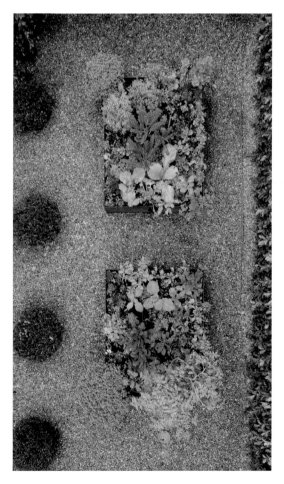

Garden Trio

My mom, the interior designer, always says to put things in groups of threes. And when I get to line up three gardens in a row, I see why. When a space is very long or more circular, creating a garden in a group of three is a great way to maximize the space. I've created a garden trio twice for myself, first in our driveway garden in Houston and now I have six gardens, essentially two garden trios, along the side of my home in the Chicago area.

Mom, can you believe I finally listened to you?

If your garden space is longer than it is wide, or if it's more circular and curved, a garden trio may be a perfect solution.

Four-Garden Classic

If you have a space that's square, or nearly square, in shape and at least 15 feet wide (4.6 m), a four-garden classic is my favorite option. Functionally, four distinct gardens give you the option of separating crops and plants more methodically. And aesthetically, four gardens are absolute perfection in terms of kitchen garden design.

The feeling you'll have inside your four-garden classic is magical and truly an escape from reality (which is not a bad thing in the middle of a busy work week).

Formal Potager

And if your landscape allows for a total garden area that's more than 20 feet (6.1 m) wide and long, you have space to create a formal *potager*. These designs are so large and ornate we had to call in the French language to help us describe them.

Potagers go well beyond a few raised gardens and include additional features such as fountains, fruit trees, seating areas, and more. I've had the opportunity to design a handful of formal potagers and the experience and transformation were a privilege.

Potagers include garden beds with unique angles and curves and the gardens work together to create something of a maze or enclosure. If your space is ready for a formal potager, hiring a garden consultant is a great idea.

Now it's your turn to create a layout that maximizes your growing space and suits your landscape. Think about your home and landscape and tie your garden to your space.

FIVE GARDEN LAYOUTS

Border Garden
» For limited space or to preserve the yard for other uses
» Minimum of 2 feet (0.6 m) of width available

Twin Gardens
» For rectangular spaces in the main lawn
» Minimum of 13 feet (4 m) of width available

Garden Trio
» For a long or circular space
» Minimum of 15 feet (4.6 m) of width available

Four-Garden Classic
» For square or nearly square garden areas in the main lawn
» Minimum of 15 feet (4.6 m) of width available

Formal Potager
» For larger spaces and additional features
» Minimum of 20 feet (6.1 m) of width and length available

Site Requirements

As you think about your garden layout, keep these numbers in mind:

LENGTH: the longer the garden the more you'll need to support the garden bed internally. We've found the maximum size is about 15 feet (4.6 m) long for one continuous garden and the magic length is between 6 and 8 feet (1.8 and 2.4 m).

WIDTH: The width of a raised bed, if accessible from all sides, should be no more than 4½ feet (1.4 m) wide (we can make an exception if we have large trellises through the garden's center and extend it to 5 feet [1.5 m]). If the garden is only accessible from one side, you'll want to max out at 3 feet (0.9 m), which is a—literal—stretch. Two to 2½ feet (0.6 to 0.8 m) wide is pretty much the standard for a border garden. You'll find that your arms, in general, will only reach 2½ feet (0.8 m) into the garden, unless you've got elastic arms (in which case I'd love to hire you!).

HEIGHT: For the height of a garden, start with a minimum of 6 inches (15.2 cm). This height will really only accommodate greens and herbs. Generally, we start with at least 1 foot (0.3 m) for garden height and may go up as high as 2½ feet (0.8 m) depending on the client's needs and the surrounding structure. Note: most of our gardens are right at 2 feet (0.6 m) tall.

PATHWAYS AND BORDERS: Pathways should be 2 to 3 feet (0.6 to 0.9 m) wide. A wheelbarrow generally measures about 2 feet (0.6 m) wide. For border garden pathways, they only need to be about 1½ to 2 feet (0.5 to 0.6 m) wide.

Summary

I mean, how many decisions could I force you to make in one chapter? If you suffer from analysis paralysis (me, too!) this hasn't been your favorite part.

Now it's time to use the layout you've selected and the size and shape that fits your budget, time, and output desires, and pencil your kitchen garden onto your map. After you've completed this process, it may be a little more obvious why Gardenary and Rooted Garden exist. The process of kitchen garden design can be a little daunting. But now that you've learned more about your property and its needs and characteristics, you're well on your way to that kitchen garden you desire. And, if you need a little more clarity, you can always get direction and find your own garden coach to help you at gardenary.com.

After drawing your garden design onto the map, it's time to step out and stake the garden. This will help you determine if you've chosen the right spot.

STAKING THE GARDEN

Staking the garden will help you better envision what the finished kitchen garden will look and feel like. For this project, you'll first mark off the entire garden area, including all borders and pathways—not just the raised gardens—and then measure your garden beds from that exterior edge.

What You'll Need

- Heavy mallet
- Wooden stakes (1 for each corner of the garden and 1 for each corner of every raised bed)
- Twine
- Scissors
- Exterior spray paint (optional)

1. Mark off the entire garden area by placing a stake at each corner of the garden area and either spraying the entire perimeter with paint or using twine between the stakes to delineate the area. Each raised bed edge will be measured from these outer lines to ensure that the beds are symmetrical and aligned.

2. Measure the distance necessary from the marked outer border to the corner of the first raised bed and hammer a stake into that spot.

3. Return to the garden area's outer edge (marked with paint) and measure the correct distance from the outer edge to mark the remaining three corners of the same raised bed.

4. Once all four stakes are placed, use twine to connect the stakes to form what will eventually become the raised garden shape.

5. After you've staked the first raised garden bed, use the outer garden area lines to measure and stake the second and all other raised beds (as needed) in the same fashion. Once complete, you'll be able to see the shape the garden beds will take within your landscape.

The installed reality of a kitchen garden can be difficult to imagine when it's only on graph paper. Staking the garden area before installation gives you a sense of what's coming and whether the design is heading in the right direction. Once you've staked the garden, adjust it as needed and, before long, those stakes will be replaced with beautiful garden beds.

CHAPTER TWO
GATHER

Select Your Kitchen Garden Elements

● ● ● ● ● ●

How many embarrassing stories should I share about gathering the materials for a kitchen garden with you? Since 2015, my first company, Rooted Garden has installed more than 100 custom kitchen gardens (and still counting) and every beautiful garden has a story to go with it.

Should I tell you about that time I tried to load 12-foot-long (3.7 m) cedar planks into my minivan and ended up busting out my front windshield? Or maybe about that time I put so many bags of soil into my van that the back bumper was nearly dragging on the concrete on my way to the client? What about when a steel bed arrived and it was so heavy it took more than six men to carry it? Or, that day I over-ordered plants for a client and my children had to ride home from school with tomatoes, peppers, and flowers in their laps?

Should we talk about trellises? There was that one time I decided I didn't need to read the directions on the arch trellis only to have it stuck together the wrong way. And I had no option but to ask my clients to jump in and help me pull it apart. Or, that time the trellis was just too narrow to fit between the two beds so we, literally, had to saw off the ends.

I've made all the mistakes in terms of gathering materials for a kitchen garden. But good news: You don't have to.

A beautiful kitchen garden at the season's peak can seem like it's made of a million things. But underneath the overflowing herbs, vining tomatoes, and bright flowers, are just four key structures. These essentials include raised beds, trellises, borders, and pathways. Rooted Garden's signature system always includes these four elements in each kitchen garden design and you should, too.

Four Structures

If you haven't noticed already, all the gardens pictured here are made up of raised gardens. With few exceptions, raised beds are all we do.

RAISED BEDS provide the ideal growing conditions for herbs and vegetables. By building raised gardens, you'll create a form and structure for your kitchen garden that's as productive as it is attractive. When done right (and yours will surely be), raised gardens provide the optimal soil, temperature, and water conditions for picky vegetable and herb plants. Although gardening directly in the ground is possible and can be productive, it may take years to slowly amend a row of soil before great output can be expected. But with raised beds, you begin with ideal conditions and then just work to keep them that way.

TRELLISES provide year-round vertical interest in a garden but also offer much needed support for your flourishing tomatoes and bean vines. In the height of growing season, trellises are covered with green but, even in the coldest season, when everything else may be dormant, the trellis's structure will keep the kitchen garden attractive and interesting.

BORDERS help distinguish your kitchen garden from the rest of your yard and landscape. Because the kitchen garden should be a distinct section of your yard, the border ensures this is the case—both aesthetically and functionally. When done right, the border will prevent weeds and other parts of the landscape from creeping into the garden space.

PATHWAYS make walking into your garden a convenient and welcoming experience. As you step over the threshold to the kitchen garden, you'll feel like you're escaping the rest of the world.

watercolors

note cards

sketch paper

larger graph paper

ruler

idea book

pen and pencil

Over the years, these four structures have become the standard for every kitchen garden I, and my company, design. No matter the space or layout, these four structures work together to create a complete and practical setup. Trust me: it works.

So, let's gather the four structures for your kitchen garden.

Before You Start

Before you start, it's important to establish an overall style for your space. Aim to create a space that looks like it's been part of your home and landscape from the very beginning. One of the best compliments I receive in my work is to hear someone say, "The garden looks like it's always been there." To accomplish this in your garden, it's important to, first, recognize the established style of your home and landscape.

My first official garden consult was with Jenny. Her gray stucco home was gorgeous. I was greeted with beautiful patina wood planters in front, a gorgeous dark stained wooden door, and a wrought iron gate covered in ivy that led me to the backyard.

"I'd love the garden to have a 'French' feel to it."

I nodded my head, pretending I knew what she meant. I'd studied French in middle school, high school, and college. I could *parlez Français* enough to order a croissant, so I should certainly know what making a kitchen garden look "French" meant, right?

Not exactly.

This new modern home needed a modern garden design outside the back door.

A stucco garden trimmed with stained cedar fits perfectly in this Spanish colonial home setting.

Little did I know I was standing in the middle of the answer. Jenny's home already had a "French" appeal. And she was just asking me to create a garden that was a continuation of her existing style.

Extending your home's style into the garden is what you'll do, too (no French needed).

Just as Jenny used the word "French," you'll need to select a word that your architect or the neighborhood development would use to describe the style of your home, apartment, or condominium. This could be modern, farmhouse, traditional, Mediterranean, mid-century, or, perhaps, French. I've lived in a row home in Pennsylvania, a traditional home in Tennessee, a ranch home in Texas, and now a modern farmhouse in the Chicago area.

If you're completely stuck (like I've been before) and can't think of a word to describe the existing style of your home, create an online search on your home's specific elements. Use words to describe your home's construction materials, architectural features, the decade of your home's construction, or even the shape of your roof. As you search for these features, you'll begin to find suggestions of styles that include these elements. And, soon, you'll discover (and appreciate) the existing style of your home.

A year later, though I'd matched quite a few gardens and home styles, I met a wonderful client with a home style I couldn't name. The exterior walls were stucco, the roof was made with clay tile, and the windows included ornate iron elements. I did what any smart girl would do. I called my mom. When I named the three elements, she knew the style right away: Spanish colonial. And, of course, Mom was right. I used this style and theme to guide me through each step in the garden design process.

Once you've defined your home's style, you'll use that word as a check on your selections of each kitchen garden element. If your home has a clean and modern feel, be certain to design a kitchen garden that feels the same. Does your home include an Eastern influence? Let's be sure to have some in the garden, too. Traditional? You're going to need a traditional garden structure.

This alignment with your home's existing style is one key way the kitchen garden differs from a sprawling veggie patch. By incorporating your home's design, the kitchen garden becomes an extension—and, even, a central feature of your home and landscape. Taking a few minutes now to consider the style of your home will give you a guiding principle that can keep you focused and narrow your decisions in the chapters to come.

And, in a few months, when your friends come for a walk through your kitchen garden and tell you it looks like it's always been there, you'll know you've done it right.

Measuring the Garden

But before you can get the compliment, you've got to gather your supplies. If you're building your beds, re-measure your shape and size plan (see page 42) to ensure you'll be gathering the right amount of wood, steel, or stone. This is a great time to hire help or get an expert to assist you.

These are numbers you'll want to keep in your garden journal:

» Measure the entire perimeter of your kitchen garden space. This is two times the length and two times the width of the entire space devoted to your kitchen garden project.

» Multiply the width by the length of the *entire garden space* to know the total garden area square footage.

» List the length and width of *each raised garden bed*. Multiply the length and width of each bed and add them to know the total raised garden bed square footage.

» Finally, determine the total cubic footage of your garden space by multiplying the square footage of each bed by its height. (L x W x H). This will give you the total cubic footage of your kitchen garden beds.

Raised Beds

Though you can certainly have a kitchen garden without a raised bed, I wouldn't recommend it. Raised beds produce such reliable results, provide a stunning look in the yard, and create consistency throughout the seasons that helps stabilize the kitchen garden area even as plants rise and fall.

You can create your raised beds with a wide variety of materials. The key aspect to prioritize for raised beds is that the material is natural, durable, beautiful, and sustainable.

And, yes, Dad, I suppose, there is that issue of whether it's affordable.

Natural

We prioritize natural garden beds because our goal is to create an organic environment for our edible plants as possible. Always source materials as close to their naturally occurring state as possible. Our favorite materials to use are untreated wood, steel that hasn't been coated with synthetic chemicals, and stone that hasn't been chemically altered.

Durable

Though using natural products is the goal with our raised beds, you'll also want to be certain your raised bed material is durable. Your beds will be asked to endure all sorts of weather and challenges, and you'll want gardens that can stand up to the elements. Untreated wood, clearly, has a limited lifetime but using woods such as cedar, redwood, cypress, or hemlock can prolong the garden's life expectancy by five or ten years. Steel can last for decades, but you'd want its exterior to be treated with a rust protectant. Finally, stone is clearly going to last for, pretty much, ever after.

Beautiful

Because your kitchen garden will be an extension of your home and landscape, you'll want to tend to the aesthetics of it. An aspect of matching your garden to your home's style is selecting a material that aligns with your home's existing structures.

Sustainable

Though it's not always easy to measure, it's also important to consider sustainably sourced materials for your garden. When shopping for hardwood, try to source from trees that have been sustainably harvested and check to see if the miller replants trees after harvest. For steel or metal, ask how far the material has traveled and about the excavating process. For stone, choose materials that come naturally from your area, whenever possible.

Affordable

My dad would want me to tell you to choose a raised bed material that works for your budget. Although cedar is an expensive wood, it's generally the least expensive of our recommended raised bed materials. Steel and metal gardens are next in affordability and stone gardens will be the most expensive, if installed with a cement footer. I've also included clay and cloth as affordable options in the chart below.

Material	Natural	Durable	Beautiful	Sustainable	Affordable
Wood	⇉	⇉	⇉	⇉	⇉
Metal		⇉	⇉		
Stone	⇉	⇉	⇉		
Cloth	⇉			⇉	⇉
Clay	⇉	⇉		⇉	⇉

Wood

Wood is the least expensive and one of the easiest ways to get started with your kitchen garden. Use untreated wood but one that won't decay quickly, such as cedar, redwood, or hemlock. The best choice will differ based on your geographical location, so be sure to find the most locally sourced wood you can. And once you've selected your wood source, aim to buy the thickest pieces of wood you can afford to improve durability.

To create a wooden garden like the Gardenary signature bed, you'll need to purchase 2 × 6-inch × 8-foot (5.2 × 15.2 cm × 2.4 m) boards for the bed structure as well as 1 × 4-inch × 8-foot (2.5 × 10.2 cm × 2.4 m) boards for the trim.

Wait, let me translate the numbers for you.

» The first number for a lumber measurement is the board thickness in inches (cm).

» The second number is the board height (in inches [cm] as well).

» The final number is the board length in feet (m).

In fact, our ideal piece of wood, based on its availability, affordability, and durability, is a 2 × 6-inch × 8-foot (5.2 × 15.2 cm × 2.4 m) cedar plank. So, practice saying, "two by six by eight" and then head to the hardware store and place your order.

To know the amount of boards you'll need, calculate it with this equation, refer to the raised bed cubic footage you calculated earlier in this chapter (see page 49)—assuming you did calculate it. If not, now's the time!

BEST WOOD TYPES FOR GARDENS

Wood Type	Location
Cedar	Midwestern United States, Mediterranean region, Europe
Cypress	Southern and Eastern United States
Hemlock	Canada
Ironwood	South and Central America
Mahogany	Africa
Redwood	Western United States
Teak	Southern and Southeast Asia

You'll multiply the length × the width of your bed × the height of your garden. That's the simple calculation to know how much wood you'll need.

If you're building more than a few gardens, it's worthwhile to seek out a local lumberyard. When purchasing wood, take time to pull out each board separately and inspect it. Look for discoloration or any defects. And, most importantly, check each board for straightness. The longer the board, the more likely there's a curve. These are natural products, after all. Be certain you find the straightest boards possible. Once you've secured your boards, check your measurements to be certain you have the right amount of wood.

Finally, have the store cut your lumber so you can skip that step at home, if you're certain of your bed measurements. This ensures the cut will be straighter and enables you to build a squarer bed. (Hint: I do this all the time).

If you'd like to find a kitchen garden company to construct the beds for you, you can search our index at gardenary.com, or simply call some carpenters. There are also raised garden kits online, but I suggest you beware of many as the wood is often quite thin. I carry a few raised garden kits with appropriate thicknesses in my online store. If you can't find the measurement for the thickness of the wood online, head to a local store instead.

Steel

One of the first small kitchen gardens I installed was a repurposed water trough made of stainless steel. I made two of these for our client by adding drainage holes and casters to the bottom. I've created loads of small lettuce and herb planters from stainless steel containers—both small and large—but the real treat was creating custom Corten planters for a few clients. Corten is a brand name that's now standard for describing

steel that forms a stable rust appearance. After starting with Corten, Rooted Garden has also designed several powder-coated steel gardens.

Although steel is made from mined iron, it's been proven to be quite a sustainable resource, as it can always be completely recycled. Some steel may be treated with zinc for durability but there's little to no chance this will affect the organic nature of your soil.

Steel gardens will, literally, last a lifetime—and then some. And one thing I love about garden beds made with steel is the small footprint of the bed itself. If you're growing in a small space and want to maximize your growing area, a steel bed enables you to give nearly all the space to your plants while still having a super strong garden bed that will never give up growing.

Stone

Another beautiful option we use for bed materials is stone. Though I did a few dry lay stone gardens (where stone is not secured with cement but stacked on a sand foundation), the more durable design requires a cement footer under the stone beds.

When the cement footers are laid, you realize the significance of the space you're creating: This garden will literally be here for generations to come. There are, of course, less permanent ways to use stone. You can do something as basic as cement blocks, or chose bricks, landscape stone, or natural rock and dry stack the stones or use minimal cement.

Owning a stone garden is an item on my bucket list. But because of the expense, I may have to wait until my four kids are out of college and married and no longer asking for money for that to happen. Will that day ever come? Who knows? But in the meantime, I'll live vicariously through our clients and, maybe, you!

If it's on your bucket list, too, you can make it happen in a variety of ways. Perhaps the simplest of which is to just simply stack cement pavers on a leveled sand bed. Be certain to stabilize the stones so you get to enjoy the longevity factor instead of quickly seeing your stones crack or turn crooked with age.

Once you know your garden shape and size and you determine the material you'd like to use, it's time to gather your raised bed supplies. If you're building your beds, re-measure your shape and size plan to ensure you gather the right amount of wood, steel, or stone. This is a great time to hire help or get an expert to assist you.

Trellises

Now that you've decided on your garden layout and material, it's time to consider the trellises. I've learned the hard way not to wait until the garden is installed to add the trellises. There has been one too many times we've had to dig loads of soil out of the garden to retrofit the massive structures—and trust me: It's not fun.

Trellises help with airflow, maximize the growing space, and keep your vining plants healthy. And bonus—they're beautiful. You've just got to have some.

Trellises may just be my favorite thing in the garden. During my family's first year growing tomatoes, we did what everyone does: We purchased tomato cages from the hardware store. And, in just a matter of weeks, the cages were bursting and falling over not able to support or contain the tomato plants. I knew I needed a different solution.

The following season, I scavenged for bamboo sticks and, brought dozens home from my parents' town in Mississippi (minivan to the rescue). We lined them up in the garden and tied the tomatoes to the sticks with twine. But, once again, the plants overwhelmed the structure and the trellis was finished after just one season.

PLANTS *that* Need TRELLISES *Each* SEASON

Cool Season: Peas and runner beans

Warm Season: Cucumbers, pole beans, tomatoes, winter squash

Hot Season: Eggplants, tomatillos, yard-long beans

By the time I installed my first formal kitchen garden for a client, I'd learned my trellis lessons and knew I needed something different. That's when I started using metal trellises. Once placed in the garden, I realized what a statement each metal trellis made. The vertical interest completely changed the garden's feel and, when covered with those previously sprawling tomato vines, they were absolute kitchen garden magic.

TYPE *of* TRELLIS *and* GARDEN

PANEL: Border and narrow gardens

OBELISK: Wide and central gardens

ARCH: Twin gardens and four-garden classic

Look for trellises made from steel that will resist rust and discoloration. To start, you can begin with bamboo or wooden trellises, but, take it from me, those wooden trellises will rarely last more than a season or two.

The plants that need trellises are those that grow with a vining habit or grow so tall they tend to fall over in strong wind, rainstorms, or, better yet, the weight of the fruit they're holding.

In the cool season, peas and runner beans need a trellis to climb and, in the warm season, cucumber vines, pole beans, and winter squash benefit from growing on a trellis. In the hot season, certain types of cucumbers and beans will grow on a trellis.

There are other vining plants that benefit from the support of a trellis. Nearly all members of the Solanaceae family require support of some type (see chapter 5 for more on plant families). And I've always enjoyed growing indeterminate (vining) tomatoes on trellises. This allows the plant to grow larger and makes it much simpler to prune and tend than those in a traditional tomato cage. In the hot season, tomatillos benefit from hanging onto a trellis as well.

Trellises, essentially, come in three different shapes (at least according to me): panel, obelisk, and arch.

When selecting a trellis, look for those with thin wires that small pea and cucumber tendrils can grab easily. Also look for only small breaks from one section of the trellis to the next. Most plants will gain just a few inches of growth from week to week and will need a new rung to cling to at each stage. Trellises should range from 6 to 8 feet (1.8 to 2.4 m) tall, unless you're a pro basketball point guard, in which case you could stretch it to 9 or 10 feet (2.7 to 3 m). You can use shorter trellises (4 to 5 feet [1.2 to 1.5 m]) to support peppers, eggplants, or bush tomatoes (more on that in chapter 7), but, for vining plants, the trellis needs to be taller.

Panel

Panel trellises are tall, flat structures and are the simplest type for the kitchen garden. Panels are great for border gardens as they allow you to maximize your growing space by sending your vines up along the wall or fence beside which you've placed your garden. We love using panel trellises along a fence line, a garage, or the home itself. We've also used panel trellises down the middle of a wide bed. In this case, you can grow along both sides of the trellis.

The simplest panel trellis to use is a cattle panel, which can be found at farm supply stores, but we've enjoyed using panels that make more of a stylistic statement as well.

Obelisk

Obelisk trellises are great for adding height and unique interest in the middle of a garden bed. Obelisks have a triangular shape and are best suited for square or rectangular gardens in either the corners or the middle of the beds. They work well in the center of wider gardens and provide a great deal of room for planting around the base, but plants do get a bit crowded as the trellis comes to a point at the top. Obelisk trellises are great inside a border garden, in the center of two or more gardens on a four garden classic, or even in all four corners of a formal potager.

Arch

Arch trellises are a wonderful addition to the twin garden, four-garden classic, or formal potager designs. The arch allows for growing between gardens and maximizing your garden space. Arch trellises must be secured well at the base of the trellis as a lot of weight will be placed on the middle of the arch. Arches are wonderful for allowing plants to grow as tall as they'd like. As the vines pass over the upper corner of the arch, they're able to grow across the top and back down, if the season allows it. If you have a long growing season and want your tomatoes to grow as big and long as possible, an arch trellis is a great option.

Gather your trellises before you install your kitchen garden. Placing the trellis in your garden before the soil is completely installed will help ensure they're secure in their spot, especially if your gardens are deep.

Now it's your turn: Scavenge the neighborhood for some bamboo or assemble an ornate arch trellis. It's up to you! But, whatever you do, learn from my mistakes and skip the tomato cages.

Borders

The word, "borders" sounds a lot like "boring" right?

And it may feel that way, but a garden's borders are more important than you'd think. Borders play both an aesthetic and a practical role in your kitchen garden. The garden edges keep it separate from the rest of the landscape. If you have lawn or grass or other vegetation growing near your kitchen garden area, a strong material border is important to keep that vegetation from heading into your garden space. It may seem to have nothing to do with the kitchen garden of your dreams but setting your garden apart now may be one of the most critical steps to ensuring a tidy and beautiful garden for years to come.

Create clean lines in your landscape and denote the important and unique part of your yard that is the kitchen garden. Remember the definition of a kitchen garden is that it's a distinct segment of your landscape—a spot set apart—and a border does just that.

You'll set up the border first, so it's important to order or gather your border material early in the process. You can create borders with stone, brick, bushes, or landscape material, or simply use steel edging. We also use sidewalks and driveways to help provide borders for the garden.

To calculate the amount of material you'll need for the border, refer to the perimeter measurement you took at the beginning of this chapter. This measurement includes all the surrounding edges of the gardens, the pathways, and any other feature that would add to the measurement of the whole space. If using steel edging, measure the perimeter distance and divide it by the length of each steel edging piece. You can generally get edging in 10-foot (3 m) pieces but, with edges overlapping, that will only cover about 8 feet (2.4 m). So, measure accordingly.

Options for Borders

Steel, Rubber or Composite Edging

Decorative Borders

Brick or Stone

Pathways

Have you ever enjoyed visiting a place but the road to get there was such a pain to travel you didn't want to go back? Maybe it's just me but I'm so much more likely to head to a place when I know there's not a high likelihood of hitting traffic or road construction. Otherwise, I'm staying home.

This is why pathways in your kitchen garden are so important. This is your new special place; remember? So, let's clear the way to get there. With garden pathways, consider the measurements of the space, the material underfoot, and any other features included in the garden area.

The goal is to be able to walk comfortably between the gardens, to be able to stand and work alongside your raised beds without bumping into anything. Common wheelbarrows measure 2 to 3 feet (0.6 to 0.9 m) in width, so we generally aim for about 3 feet (0.9 m) between gardens—and no more, unless the beds are quite large (we're talking formal potager kind of large). If you're creating a border garden, I suggest providing at least 1 foot (0.3 m) of pathway along the side of the garden so you're not standing awkwardly in wet sod, or dirt, or halfway onto the garden area and halfway off.

Rooted Garden designs almost always use gravel for the pathway material. Gravel works both functionally and aesthetically in the garden space. In terms of a pathway, gravel provides a clean area that will be free of weeds and other vegetation; it drains quickly; and requires little upkeep. Gravel also provides a way for you to level your kitchen garden beds,

Limestone

Crushed Granite

Pea Gravel

Crushed Rock

Stone Chips

Stone Screenings

River Rock

which can be a challenge otherwise. Finally, gravel provides added protection for your raised garden bed as it keeps your bed, particularly wood bed, from sitting on soft or wet dirt or sod. This prolongs the life of your gardens by years.

There are other materials you can use, such as pine straw, moss, turf, or stone, but my recommendation is gravel.

A common garden often has mulch between garden beds. And although that solution can work well for pathways, I don't recommend using it unless you must. This is for two reasons: Mulch will continuously decompose (needing a new installment once a year) and my experience has shown that pests love to hide in the mulch. If you do use mulch, my recommendation is pine straw instead of hardwood mulch. Pine straw won't attract as many pests and won't decompose as quickly. But, if you have the budget, I highly recommend the gravel instead.

As part of the pathway, you may want to include stepping stones. Though gravel is practical and makes the garden space clean, it's not the best for bare feet. For this reason, many of our clients opt to add large stepping-stones to the garden area. These stones should be ordered and secured at this stage so they can be leveled appropriately with gravel around them. Be sure to pick stones large enough to hold your entire foot at once (minimum 1 foot [30.5 cm] in length). And be certain to do the math to ensure you have enough stones to create a symmetrical distribution throughout the garden pathways.

HOW *to* CALCULATE GRAVEL

Length of garden area × width of garden area = total garden area

Total garden area / 4 = total gravel cubic feet

Total gravel cubic feet of gravel / 27 = total yard requirements of gravel

If yardage less than 1, use bags

If yardage greater than 1, order a truck

Summary

It's now time to check all your measurements and place your orders. Gathering your materials is great retail therapy for the one who loves shopping and a total trap for someone who hates making decisions. If you get stuck, ask for help and don't linger on any one decision too long. Take advice from my dad who's a pro at making decisions: If you have most things right, everything will turn out alright. In other words, don't sweat the small stuff. Gather your energy, your courage, your checkbook, all the garden photos, and order your materials. Nothing will push you forward like a beautiful trellis or a fragrant piece of wood sitting in your yard. And the story you create from the experience will be one of the best parts of the process.

CHAPTER THREE

FRAME

Install the Kitchen Garden Structures

● ● ● ● ●

If you're feeling a bit nervous at this point, I can relate. My heart is always beating a bit faster on garden installation day. Always. When the soil company clerk calls to tell me they're heading out and will be dumping several tons of soil at our clients' home, or when the team begins digging up sod, when I'm loading my van with plants, and, especially, when the whole area is torn up and there's nothing new growing yet, I'm crossing my fingers and quietly whispering, "I hope this turns out okay."

The butterflies are there for a reason. There's a lot at stake here.

If it can go wrong, it has. Not enough soil or way too much (I'm talking *waaaay* too much), a trellis that arrives broken, or never comes at all, a garden bed 1 foot (0.3 m) too big for the space (that was a rough day), or a bad pathway estimation, which means it's time to move those 100-pound (45.3 kg) stepping stones— for the third time. Yes, I have faced all these frustrations and mistakes—in a single season.

Let me tell you some words I repeat to myself when I get a little overwhelmed with a new garden project: "Worse First."

As you start to remove the existing plants and structures in your kitchen garden area, everything is going to feel a little overwhelming and scary. It's going to look worse first.

Keep these words in mind as you begin to frame your garden and hang in there when you hit bumps and frustrations, knowing I've been there too. We're going to make a little mess together but after it gets worse, it's going to get so much better. Let's begin!

Frame Garden Boxes

Before you circle a date on the calendar for the garden installation, be certain you have your raised beds selected and ready for the garden space. Of course, if you're building a stone garden, those will need to be constructed in place, but wood and steel beds can be prepared beforehand.

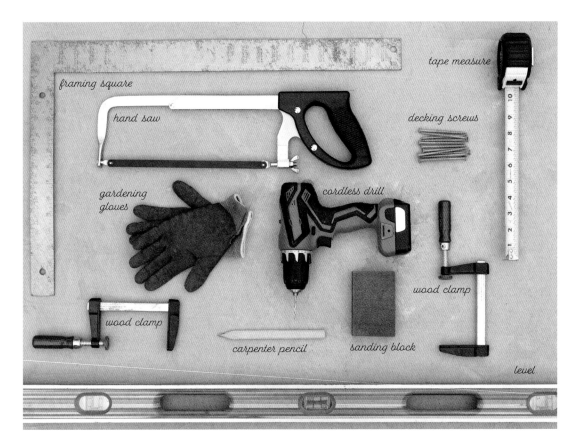

framing square

hand saw

tape measure

decking screws

gardening gloves

cordless drill

wood clamp

wood clamp

carpenter pencil

sanding block

level

How to Build a Garden Box

For one of my first large installations, (a four-garden classic), I had cedar kits ready to assemble at the job site. I'd hired a crew to handle the installation and planned to construct the beds while they worked. But, from the beginning, I realized I should've had the beds assembled beforehand. We needed the beds to be set out on the existing landscape to confirm the garden area calculations and to be certain I'd ordered enough soil. Having the gardens ready to go would have also meant I could focus completely on the garden setup details, which was moving more quickly than anticipated (this team worked much faster than my husband and I!).

So, lesson here: Have your raised beds constructed and ready to put into place before you start tearing up your garden area.

I have to admit that constructing a raised garden is one of the more challenging aspects of installing a kitchen garden, especially if you're not accustomed to working with wood and tools.

But, if you can't already tell: I'm never one to shy away from a challenge. (And I'm guessing you're not either).

For one of my first installations, I needed to measure and cut wood on site. So, I did what every sane woman would do: I headed to the hardware store and bought myself an

Materials Needed

» 2 x 6-inch x 8-foot (5.1 x 15.2 cm x 2.4 m) cedar planks

» 1 x 6-inch x 8-foot (2.5 x 15.2 cm x 2.4 m) cedar trim (optional)

» 1½-inch (3.8 cm) deck screws

» 1-inch (2.5 cm) finishing screws

Tools Needed

» Sanding paper

» Framing square

» Drill

» Mallet

» Saw

» Pencil

» Measuring tape

» Safety glasses

» Gloves

electric saw. As soon as Jason came home, he looked at me with fear in his eyes and quickly canceled all our evening plans. He spent the next few hours coaching me on the dos and don'ts of playing with saws. I'm proud to say I still have all ten fingers (at least at the time of this writing), but I was ready to let someone else do the cutting and construction for me after he explained what could possibly go wrong.

So, whether it's you, someone you love, or someone you've hired, here are the general steps to constructing a garden box from wood.

STEP-BY-STEP INSTALLATION

1. Construct the raised beds

2. Clear and cover (begin irrigation)

3. Add borders

4. Fill pathways

5. Add and align raised beds

6. Add and level trellises

7. Fill raised beds

To start, measure the thickness of your wood. Keep in mind that as you connect the boards, you'll be adding the thickness of two long boards to every short board. This means you'll need to subtract twice the board's thickness from the total length of the short board before cutting.

For example, if your boards are 1½ inches (3.8 cm) thick and you're creating a 4 × 6-foot (1.2 × 1.8 m) garden, you'll need to cut two sides of the garden at 6 feet (1.8 m) long and the other two sides at 3 feet, 9 inches (0.9 m, 22.9 cm). Confused? Hang in there!

Now that you know the measurement for the long boards and the adjusted measurement for the short ones, measure your boards to the correct dimensions and mark the cutting line on each. Be certain all beds of the same measurement line up well with one another.

After cutting the boards, it's time to connect them. Use 1½-inch (3.8 cm) screws to connect the long boards to both sides of a short board so the angles are straight and flush. Build each complete box separately before connecting them, ensuring the corners meet at a right angle every time. If you've followed my suggestion and purchased 6-inch (15.2 cm)-wide boards, you'll need two complete boxes for every foot (0.3 m) of your raised garden bed. For example, there should be two layers if you're building a 1-foot (0.3 m) garden and three layers if you're building an 18-inch (0.5 m) garden.

Once you've created all your boxes, stack all the layers and attach them: Drill down from the top of each layer to the one below it and then connect them with a 1½-inch (3.8 cm) screw. Do this at every corner.

Then, reinforce the connection by attaching a trim piece measured to the height of the garden box in the center of each panel. Secure the reinforcement with 1½-inch (3.8 cm) screws.

If you'd like, add trim to the corners and tops of your garden boxes. You can trim the garden with any board width, but we generally use a 1 × 6-inch (2.5 × 15.2 cm) board. This is optional but gives a finished, more traditional look. If you've chosen a more modern or simple style for your garden, leave the gardens as is.

ASSEMBLING GARDEN BOXES

1. Collect the cedar boards.

2. Measure and cut the long and short boards to size.

3. Connect each layer of the long and short boards to one another.

4. Stack the beds on top of one another and screw each layer together.

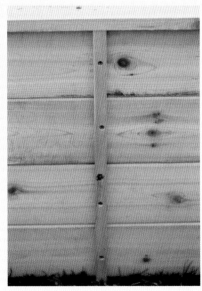

5. Place a support along the inside of the boxes to keep them together.

6. Create trim for the garden corners and attach it. Cut mitered edges for the top trim and attach with screws.

If this bed setup seems a wee bit too complicated for you now, I hear you. When I first began Rooted Garden, the whole company was just me, myself, and yep, still me. I was the administrator, the garden consultant, the installation crew, and maintenance crew. And this meant I was also the carpenter.

One of my first jobs had measurements that went well beyond the DIY kits I was using. So, I knew I'd have to create my own. Looking for a solution, I created a simple way to construct a garden using only a drill with a bolt tightener. I had the boards cut at the hardware store and then put the beds together in my garage. I simply drilled the holes at the corresponding spots on each end and then used framing angles (from the decking section at the hardware store) to connect each corner. Directions for this style of bed can be found at gardenary.com/book.

Steel

Steel garden boxes are a little more complicated to track down and acquire but much simpler in terms of construction because someone else has done the hard work for you (unless, on the off chance, YOU'RE the steel artist).

If ordering one yourself, double check details on the material and whether the steel has been galvanized. Steel should be prepared for the elements and able to hold up without rusting. If ordering steel gardens, be sure to ask about longevity and whether anything was added to the raw material.

The simplest form of a steel garden, which can still be so chic, is to use a feeding trough, add drainage holes, and place it on casters.

One of the first kitchen gardens I created was made this way. If you're in an urban area, the biggest challenge may be locating the steel tub (I had to drive an hour outside the city to find one). And the second challenge may be fitting one inside your car. (How many times can I test my minivan's abilities?).

But, dealing with those challenges is totally worth it.

Here's how to create a patio or deck garden with a steel tub:

HOW *to* CREATE *a* STEEL TUB GARDEN

Materials

- » Steel watering trough
- » Four 4-inch (10.2 cm) casters (holding 250 pounds [113.4 kg] each)
- » Sixteen $5/16$-inch (8 mm) hex bolts at 1½ inches (3.8 cm) each
- » 16 washers
- » 16 nuts
- » Weed barrier cloth

Tools

- » Measuring tape
- » Drill
- » Drill bit for $5/16$ inch (8 mm)
- » Drill bit for 1 inch (2.5 cm)
- » Safety goggles
- » Gloves

To create this trough garden, start by marking the holes for the casters.

1. Mark proper holes for the casters at each corner.

2. Drill each hole.

3. Connect the casters to each corner of the bed with washers and nuts.

4. Drill 1-inch (2.5 cm) drainage holes every square foot (0.09 m²) inside the trough.

5. Cover the bottom of the trough with weed barrier cloth.

Other options for steel garden include ordering Corten gardens or hiring a steel artist to construct the beds for you. Double check the measurements and the steel materials before confirming your order. And then prepare for a possible long wait. Many of our custom steel gardens require several weeks before they're ready to be installed. But you know what I always say, "Good things take time."

Stone

Stone gardens are the one exception to the "have your garden boxes completely ready" rule. To create a permanent stone garden, you'll need to dig and fill a footer with cement. This ensures the stone walls won't crack or give way as the earth below it expands and contracts throughout the year. The requirements for the footer vary based on your location, the height of your boxes, and your unique weather conditions. If you want the permanence of a stone garden, this may be the perfect opportunity to call in a professional. You can build a more temporary stone garden by creating a sand base for your stone instead of cement.

Frame the Garden Area

The first garden we installed in our backyard was put in right over the grass. The strip of grass right along our driveway seemed like the perfect spot. Simple enough. We put down some cardboard where the three boxes would go and placed the garden boxes on top. We were finished. Right? I was ready to fill the beds and get planting, but my husband knew better.

Though our lawn looked level to us, the truth was, there were all sorts of rises and falls in the garden area. And as soon as the raised beds were placed on top, those changes in elevation were very evident, leaving big gaps in some places and not enough room in others. It was obvious that once filled with soil, there'd be dirt falling out everywhere.

Jason spent more than a little time placing bricks under parts of the garden here and there to see if he could somehow make the beds level. In the end, it was clear we should've done the difficult work of clearing and leveling the ground first. And then—and only then—installed the garden boxes. If done this way, we could've skipped all the frustration and moved right to the fun part.

All that is to say, learn a lesson from Jason, me, and our garden beds shimmied up by bricks: Don't skip this first step.

Once the garden boxes are ready to go, double check that you also have the rest of the supplies and tools you'll need for installation. If using gravel, order the delivery, or pick up a supply, for the base of the garden area. Also collect weed barrier cloth, 30 percent vinegar, and the border and pathway material you've selected. Having all these materials and supplies ready to go will make the most of your installation hours. If you'll be tying into a formal irrigation system or want to have your water lines hidden under your boxes, you'll need supplies ready as well. (Learn more about irrigation in chapter 4).

In chapter 1, you staked out the garden boxes. Now, it's time to stake the entire garden area. Begin by placing stakes at the four corners of the garden space. You'll remove all vegetation inside those lines so, if your measurements are a little off, now is the time to figure that out. (Ask me how I know!) It's a bit ironic to destroy what's growing in order to grow something else in its place. But remember: we're creating a distinct and central feature here and we need space to do it.

STAKE ENTIRE GARDEN AREA

Materials

» Stakes

» Twine

» Weed barrier cloth, cardboard, carpenter paper

» 30 percent vinegar

Tools

» Shovel

» Hoe

» Wheelbarrow

» Measuring tape

» Mallet

» Blowtorch (optional)

CLEAR THE AREA

1. Use a shovel or sod breaker to remove all grass or vegetation from the slaked kitchen garden area.

2. Use a rake to level the area completely.

3. Spray the area with a 30 percent vinegar solution to kill any weeds that may attempt to grow in this space (optional).

4. Cover the pathways with weed barrier cloth to ensure weeds don't return, particularly in the garden pathways.

So, consider this first step as beginning the conversation with your garden and letting it know your goals—less of that; more of this. Essentially, you're clearing the slate. If you're pulling up grass, you can always place it in a compost pile and if you're digging up bushes or other woody plants, you can replant them in other areas of the landscape or turn them into wood mulch for an ornamental part of your garden.

The stakes mark where you'll place the border and will help you check your calculation for how much gravel you'll need to cover the entire garden area. Tie twine or string between each stake to see the entire garden space more clearly and to be sure your lines remain straight as you install each garden element.

Use a hoe or shovel to dig the outer lines of the garden area and then begin to clear the area inside that perimeter. Begin on the line and work your way through the garden area, clearing it of any vegetation or other landscape pieces that stand between you and your kitchen garden plans.

If you're looking for a good arm workout, you've just found it. Sometimes, our garden installations require the muscle of four men to clear just one garden area. So, drink some water, rest, and get ready to wake up with biceps tomorrow. (I told you this gardening thing would make you healthier.)

When the shoveling gets tough, there are a few ways to make the process simpler.

1. For a large area currently covered with sod, you can rent a sod cutter to get the grass formed into strips before digging.

2. If you find the ground is just too hard to dig, wait until after a hard rain so the earth is softer and plants are easier to uproot.

3. Clear only the perimeter and interior of the actual garden beds, not the surrounding garden area (leaving grass or other vegetation to keep growing in the pathways.

4. For a slower approach, first kill the vegetation either by covering it or spraying it with a vinegar solution and give it time to begin decomposing before digging into the roots. You could do this in fall to prepare for an early spring garden installation.

With Rooted Garden, we've removed countless things such as cement blocks, palm trees, rows and rows and rows of bushes, trampolines, rocks, and even previous kitchen gardens.

At this stage, if you're tying into a formal irrigation system or want to have your water lines running under your garden beds, it's important to dig a trench and lay those lines under the garden before installing the weed barrier cloth or gravel. Remember, there's more about water in chapter 4 (I won't be mad if you skip ahead and read it now).

Once the vegetation is cleared, it's time to level the area. Sounds simple: "level the area"—kind of like, "Win the World Cup" or, "Climb Mount Everest." Okay, it's not that tough but the leveling process can be a challenge. Put the hard work in now. You will have a chance to level the area more soon with gravel, but those rocks will only cover up minimal changes in topography, not big bumps and dips. So, pull out that rake and get to work.

Now that you've done the difficult work of removing all the plants and growth, the last thing you want is to see those plants pop back up near or inside your raised gardens in the months to come.

When it comes to weeds, as the saying goes, "An ounce of prevention is worth a pound of cure." So, here's the prevention plan.

First, spray the entire area with a concentrated vinegar solution. Or, if there's a seriously invasive plant that was previously growing in the area, consider burning the area with a blowtorch. (Side note: We rarely go to these extremes with Rooted Garden but if you're dealing with incredibly persistent plant species in your area, this may be necessary).

Vegetation Removal Options	Time	Ease
Shovel entire area	Several hours	Difficult
Sod cutter	Few hours	Not as difficult
Cover and kill	Months	Easiest

The next step to preventing weeds is to cover the area with a barrier that will keep new vegetation from growing. The first cover layer should be cardboard, carpenter paper, or weed barrier cloth. My preference is using thick construction paper because it will decompose over time, but we do use weed barrier cloth in the pathways for almost all clients. Be sure to cover the entire area, leaving no open spots. You can lay paper under your garden beds and weed barrier cloth in the pathways, or simply use one medium to cover the entire area.

After covering the garden area, there may still be airborne weeds that settle in the gravel pathways or into your raised beds, but this method guarantees that weeds, for the most part, won't be a challenge for you.

Now that you've cleared and leveled the area, it's time to formalize your borders and pathways.

Frame Borders and Pathways

Remember those childhood days when you'd draw a line between your space and that of your siblings to make it clear which part of the room or car was under your dominion? No? It was just my big sister who wanted me to keep out of her space?

Well, they say good fences make great neighbors so it's time to let the kitchen garden draw its own property line to let the rest of the landscape know they may come this far, but no further.

Border

Placing the garden's border first is important, as it will help contain the gravel or mulch and provide straight lines from which to align your garden beds.

Here's the good news: Most of the hard digging is behind you.

Here's the bad news: You have more digging to do.

You began this process by digging the perimeter of your garden as you removed existing vegetation. Now, it's time to deepen that edge. Hopefully, you still have the stakes and twine in place along the garden's perimeter to be certain your lines are nice and straight along your garden border. Along the edge, you'll now deepen the original line into a trench. The trench should be as deep as necessary to secure your border material. If using a 6-inch (15.2 cm)-tall piece of steel edging, the trench should be at least 3 inches (7.6 cm) deep, or deeper if you'd like less edging to stand above ground level. If your chosen border material is stone or brick, you'll need to dig a trench that's wide enough for the stone and, again, deep enough to set the stone at your preferred height. (Fig. 1. on page 78)

After digging the trench and checking for straightness, you can now place your border material. Begin at one corner and roughly place each piece around the garden area. You may be ready to start officially installing it but roughly placing them first will save you frustration later.

Fig. 1. Dig a trench around the entire garden area border.

Fig. 2. Use necessary tools to bend steel edging for the garden corners

Fig. 3. Place the steel edging inside the trenches you've created.

Fig. 4. Secure steel edging with stakes and a heavy mallet.

For steel edging, stone, or other border materials, the corners are the trickiest to handle. By doing a practice layout of the border material, you'll be able to judge which pieces should be near the corners.

If using edging, you'll need to bend it to the shape of each corner. To do so, you'll need a steel cutter, or you can utilize the corner of a strong object to place a strong bend in the steel. (Fig. 2.) But, trust me when I say, don't bend it until you're *certain* it's the exact spot that needs bending. (This is a step that's quite hard to undo and heading back to the store to buy another piece of steel edging is not my idea of a good time). If using stone or other border material, be certain the layout works so the stones end just at the corner's edge. You may need to lengthen or shorten the total garden area edge by a few inches to make it work. (Fig. 3.)

Use a soft mallet to install the steel edging, blocks, stone, or other material, being certain to keep the same straight edge with which you began. (Fig. 4.)

Pathway

Once the edging is in place, it's time to fill the pathways. If using stepping stones or other material in your pathway, now is the time to place them. Stakes and string are, once again, your friends to help you be certain that your path is straight. Placing the pathway stones before the gravel is laid ensures that the stones are stationary and level.

Once the stepping stones are in place, it's time to fill the garden space with gravel. Believe it or not, there's not much science to filling a garden with gravel. It's simply shovel and dump. As a rule, you'll want at least 3 inches (7.6 cm) of gravel throughout the garden.

If you have friends with a wheelbarrow, or a need to show off their muscles, now is a great time to call them. Since many hands make light work, find all the extra hands you can for this heavy task.

By this point, your garden area should be completely cleared, leveled, and covered with borders and pathways. It's the true definition of a "clean slate," right? And now, finally, it's time to place your garden beds.

Frame the Garden Beds

Ever typed a document, taken a picture, or created a file only to find out it has been erased? Well, it just happened again. Though you did the hard work of staking the raised garden layout in chapter 1, your hard work is now completely deleted by gravel. So, it's time to mark your lines again. Only this time, you can do so with the actual garden beds.

Fig. 1. Measure garden layout from your home and permanent landscape first and begin placing garden beds.

Fig. 2. Measure beds' distance from one another to ensure proper spacing.

Begin your measurements from the foundational pieces of the landscape first. This includes the distance from your home, a fence line, garage, or other permanent structure. Once you place the beds the correct distance from those spots, you'll then measure from the lines you created with your borders.

After placing all the garden beds, double check that the measurements are equal for each bed in a row or set. Check measurements from the front to the back of the garden to ensure the gardens are the same distance from one another all along the line. (Fig. 1 and 2.)

Once all the beds are in their spots, it's time to level the beds (yes, I know, win another World Cup). Be certain the beds are level from front to back, side to side, and with one

Fig. 3. Check to be sure each garden bed is level and that the beds are level with one another.

Fig. 4. Make adjustments by digging and adding gravel material.

Fig. 5. Confirm garden box layout.

another. (Fig. 3.) To adjust the level, you can remove or add gravel in the spots where the beds need to be raised or lowered. (Fig. 4 and 5.) Remember Jason using those bricks? This is much simpler.

This is, sometimes, the slowest part of the garden installation process but absolutely worthwhile. You certainly don't want to look out to your kitchen garden and feel as though the bed is about to fall over or, worse yet, come out after a rainstorm to find that all the seeds you so carefully planted have made their way to the lowest corner of the garden.

After this step, you're just about finished.

Set Trellises

The final step for framing out the garden is placing the trellises into the beds. Instinct would likely tell you to wait until the garden is full of soil to place your trellises. But let my experience tell your instinct that's just not a good idea. The soil you'll be filling your gardens with is quite heavy and difficult to move once placed (as you'll soon find out in the next chapter). And the trellises, especially if they're metal, are also heavy. If you wait until the end to place your trellises, you'll have difficulty getting them into the garden and the likelihood of them toppling over or not being sturdy is quite high.

So, take a moment to position your trellises where you'd like them inside the garden area. Take a step back and look at the garden with a closer eye to be sure you like all the trellis positions in the bed. Consider what the space will look like covered with vines. Beautiful right?

Use a measuring tape to be certain the trellis is placed equal distances from the garden sides, or in the same location in several different gardens. Then, use a level to be certain the rungs or levels are nice and flat. (I'm not obsessed with leveling or anything.)

If you're able to secure the trellises into the base of the garden area by covering the base with gravel or using stakes, do so at this time. If you're unable to secure their position, simply mark where they belong and be certain these go back into place before you start installing soil into the garden beds.

Summary

Once the trellises are lined up, you're ready for that magical thing that makes all garden dreams come true. But you'll have to wait until the next chapter to learn how to create yours. In the meantime, you can now officially uncross your fingers. You've completed the most significant part of creating your kitchen garden. Hopefully your nerves have settled and the butterflies are gone. "Worse first" is really a thing, isn't it? But it's also a great thing to know that the most difficult part is behind you and all of the wonder of growing in your kitchen garden is ahead. Well, nearly so. First, we'll have to get a little dirtier.

CHAPTER FOUR

FILL

Add Soil and Water

• • • • •

It was the summer in Nashville. The kids, then toddlers and babies, and I used a hand shovel and dug a few little holes, scattered the seeds we'd just bought on a whim, and then turned on the water hose.

"This is gonna work, right?"

We returned to the spot every day and, don't worry, we kept bringing the hose. Every day was the same: take a look, spray with the hose, look again, walk away. Five, six days, and a week passed. Still no sign of anything but dirt. I double-checked the seed package.

"It says here that the seeds will sprout in five to ten days."

We could've waited five to ten years and would've never seen a plant appear. The seeds had either rotted in the thick Tennessee clay soil, or they'd been washed away from all that spraying. Whatever the case, it wasn't working. Clearly this was a garden professional in the making.

Although the kitchen garden structures provide the foundation and architecture for your space, there really is nothing more important than the soil and water. These are the elements that will fill your garden with life and ensure you don't just have a bunch of boxes and trellises—you have sprouts and plants and, of course, delicious fresh harvests.

Chapter 4 may be a little late to say this but, the truth is, you could skip those boxes and the pathways and the trellises. But, if you cheat on the soil and water, you might as well forget the whole thing.

And you haven't read this far to quit now, so let's fill your garden with the very best soil and water possible and ensure you're not left standing with a hose, wet dirt, and nothing to show for it.

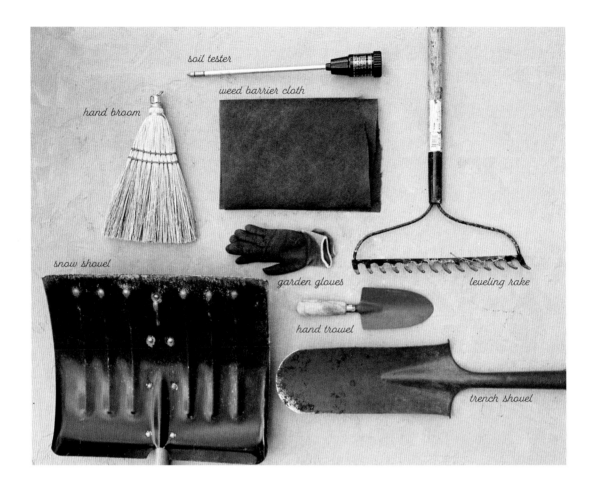

soil tester
weed barrier cloth
hand broom
snow shovel
garden gloves
leveling rake
hand trowel
trench shovel

Soil Considerations

First, let's consider the soil.

Think About Nature

When you think about the soil for your garden, take a step back and just think about nature. Profound, right?

But seriously. The bags at the hardware store, the vermiculites and perlites (and the other words you don't know how to pronounce), the peat moss, and the blends that will, supposedly, work miracles can be so confusing.

So, for a moment, forget about the store and just think about nature. If you've never stumbled upon an uncultivated berry patch or tomato vine, it may be hard to know what "nature" to think about it. So let me help.

Try to imagine a wild tomato. This tomato is growing along the banks of the Amazon River. The soil along the banks is sandy and airy and the vine is getting longer by the day. As the plant begins fruiting, some Amazonian critters (I am not sure what critters live along the Amazon River, but I'm sure they love tomatoes) come by and take a few bites. The unnamed, but very lucky, critter sits there and enjoys the tomato—leaves some skin and seeds and a little, well, you know, treasure of their own behind.

And repeat. Day after day. The vine continues to grow and fruit and be eaten by passersby until the weather turns cooler. When the night temperatures get too cold or the tomato is just tired of growing, the vines drop the remaining fruit, which then shrivel and are soon buried under the fallen leaves and plant's vine. And there you have it: a pile of dried tomatoes, leaves, dead vines, and yep, animal dung. Time passes through the cooler months and all these things slowly break down.

Then, the weather warms again. You return to that same spot a year later and, now, there's not just one, but five or ten or twenty tomato plants growing in that same spot, more lush than before. And the process begins again.

The new and fruitful tomato plants are telling you (and your imagination) that the combination of sandy, moist earth that was naturally there already, the decomposed plant and fruit matter, and the animal manure all work together to create an amazing, rich, fertile, organic soil that's perfect for growing fruits and vegetables.

And there's no spray bottle or secret ingredient necessary. Great garden soil is just a mix of nature—a combination of what's there naturally with composted materials, manures (if you can stomach it), and well-draining natural additions (like sand).

Garden soil should be second nature. You don't need to be a chemist or a horticulturist to figure it out. If you can keep this picture in mind as you set up and maintain your kitchen garden's soil, the whole thing won't feel like such a mystery.

It's obvious that the thriving tomato plant had exactly what it needed to grow. But what exactly are the main elements that make up soil in the first place?

Soil Elements

Most soils are a basic mixture of different-sized particles: sand, silt, and clay. Some soils are mostly clay or mostly sand or mostly silt, but most soils are a mixture of all three. And each of these components has a strength and a weakness to it when it comes to working in the garden.

Clay

Clay contains the smallest particles you'll find in soil. It has a high density, meaning there are lots of particles in a clay sample. It has slow permeability, meaning it holds water for a long time, and it also has little porosity. In other words, there's not a lot of air moving around in clay. On the upside, clay soils tend to have a fair amount of plant nutrients. So, although clay soil is great for holding plant roots in place, an abundance of clay is a challenge because it holds too much water and doesn't always allow air to reach the roots of your plants.

Silt

Silt has intermediate-size particles and does retain water but releases that water to the roots of nearby plants. Silt is considered the most fertile soil you can find for plants. But the challenge is its lack of ability to hold together and form a rich, crumbly structure. So, although silt can provide nutrients and better water flow for your plants than clay, it's not dense enough to hold together and support the root systems of your plants as they grow.

Sand

When compared with clay and silt, sand is made up of the largest-size particles. In fact, sand is essentially just tiny fragments of rock. The great thing about sand is that it drains quickly and easily (an essential for soils growing fruits and vegetables). But the problem with sand is it doesn't stick together and it retains very little water. This means it doesn't hold onto nutrients very well either.

Organic Matter

Organic matter is another important element of soil, though it's a small percentage of most natural soils (1 to 6 percent). In my garden soil blend, the organic matter of choice is compost. It's not just any part, it's my favorite part (and I'm pretty sure composting is going to save the planet). Compost is simply organic matter made from decomposed plant and animal materials. When compared to the other soil elements, it's made up of small to medium particles, it absorbs an enormous amount of water but drains quickly, and it holds loads of nutrients. Despite being close to perfect, compost does lack the strong structure that most vegetable roots require for good stability.

Sand	Clay	Silt	Compost
Drains Quickly	Drains Poorly	Drains but Disperses Water	Drains but Absorbs Water
Lacks Structure	Contains Structure	Lacks Structure	Lacks Structure
Lacks Nutrients	Contains Nutrients	Contains Nutrients	Contains Nutrients

Now that you know the key elements of soil, let's consider what characterizes great garden soil and start to define what already exists in your landscape or yard.

Structure

We may picture soil as a substance that can just slip through your hands, but great garden soil has a strong structure. In other words, you want your soil to hold together, at least a little bit. As your plants grow, they need a good foundation for their roots. If the space below the surface is constantly shifting or losing its shape, your plants just won't be secure. Think of a high-rise building. If the building's foundation can shift or change shape, that building won't be standing long. For this reason, you never want your garden soil to be entirely composed of sand, or even just compost (awesome as it is). Both soil components lack an enduring structure that grows strong, healthy plants.

Air

Although a strong structure is important for garden soil, a solid structure isn't. Unlike a building that needs a cement foundation as it grows tall, your plants need a strong, but open, foundation because they'll be growing both above and below simultaneously. Air pockets and pores are key to healthy garden soil, as they provide passageways for roots to grow and expand. Expanding roots mean expanding stems, leaves, and fruit—just what we want. This is why a soil mixture made mostly of clay isn't enough for your garden's soil.

Nutrients

Even if you've got a strong structure and aeration in your garden soil, you're still not quite there. Because the soil isn't just the home for your plants, it's also the restaurant. Your plants are eating here! And although they do make their own carbohydrates, thanks to photosynthesis and sunshine (plants are amazing!), they also need nutrients from the soil to create that food and grow. This is why you can't have nutrient-poor garden soil made mostly of sand. It does not provide enough nutrients to sustain your plants over their lifetime.

So, how do we get a soil blend with a strong structure, good airflow, and enough nutrients to sustain our kitchen garden plants? We create our own. My custom soil blend, which I've called the 103, is the perfect solution. At least the gardens seem to think so.

The 103 blend I've created with Rooted Garden and refer to with my online students, is my variation of "sandy loam" soil and it doesn't include anything that ends with "-lite" or is made in a lab. There are all kinds of recommendations for garden soil blends out there, but sandy loam is one of the most natural and easiest blends you can create. And after using this variation in hundreds of gardens, especially mine, I know it works.

Though you'll be creating the soil blend for your kitchen garden, it helps to know what type of soil you, mostly, have in your landscape. So, pretend you're a kid again who just wants to play in the dirt and head out to your yard and dig up a little patch.

Now hold that soil in your hands. (It's okay; I promise.) Is it a big wet clump? It's likely made of clay. Is it falling out of your hands and dry, and does it feel gritty when you rub it between your thumb and forefinger? Sounds like it's mostly sand. Or is it dark and crumbly? Then you've got either mostly silt or a high percentage of organic matter (I'll try not to be jealous). Your landscape's soil is rarely 100 percent any one element but understanding what comprises most of it will help you know how to amend it.

To create your soil blend for your kitchen garden, you have two options:

1. You can dig up soil from around your landscape and use it as a base that you'll amend for your unique kitchen garden blend.

2. Or, you can start from scratch and order an entirely new soil blend (this is what we do with Rooted Garden and Gardenary).

Amending your existing soil is less costly and, honestly, a more environmentally friendly solution. However, if you're building a significantly large garden, you may find it difficult to find enough native soil to fill the beds. The other downside is that your blend will be a little less exact if you amend your native soil. But, with either method, we have some digging to do, so let's get started.

The 103

103 percent: that's the "new math" we're about to do together. I know it doesn't sound like a real thing. But, don't worry, I took Number Theory in college so I, for sure, know what I'm talking about.

4% bonus material such as earthworm castings

33% compost full of rich organic matter

33% topsoil which adds structure to the soil blend

33% coarse sand which aids in drainage

This is my unique soil blend that's 103 percent likely to work in your kitchen garden. And it's 103 percent easier than any other soil mix out there. And, the best part? You can find all that you'll need in your town or city.

My company, Rooted Garden, has grown all our kitchen gardens based on the soil recipe I'm about to share with you. It works. It works really well. So, well I'm a little afraid to put it here on paper in case my competition is reading this . . .

It's 33 percent topsoil. This means you can use a locally sourced, commercially purchased topsoil, or you can simply dig up the top layer of soil in your existing landscape. The topsoil's main job is to be the conduit for everything else. It's like the shell for the taco. It's okay on its own, but it's at its best holding everything else that goes in it. Don't try to build a garden with just sand and compost. You need a vehicle to carry those two things. And that vehicle is topsoil.

After the topsoil you'll add about 33 percent coarse sand. Sand's main job is drainage. Nearly all edible plants hate standing in water and sand ensures that won't happen. Ever watch water move through sand at the beach? It's gone in no time, right? Sand particles are so large that the water has a million routes through it. So, when you work sand into your kitchen garden soil blend, you're ensuring the water has a million routes around and out of the garden after it does its very important job of tending to your plants' roots.

This isn't the sandbox kind of sand or the beach kind of sand but the kind of sand that builders use when doing builder sorts of projects. (It's often called "torpedo" or "carpenter" sand.) To source, you can call a local soil yard and ask them if they carry coarse sand by the yard or ton. And based on my experience, I'm pretty sure they will.

Finally—and this is the most critical piece—it's 33 percent compost. Sand and topsoil are critical, but the magic? It's in the compost. After watching compost work its magic in my garden, I started incorporating it into our clients' gardens. And the results were crazy good. Soon, compost became our magic ingredient. We use in the beginning and then we use it every season when we plant the next round of plants and seeds (more on that in the next section). Find a local supplier of compost in your area. Landscape supply centers often carry leaf compost or organic compost or mushroom compost in bulk. And good news: You can also make compost.

The addition problem 33 + 33 + 33 = not quite 100, right? Not to worry—we've got about 4 percent left. I realize I'm officially out of percentages but the point of busting 100 is to let you know it's okay to be a little extra when it comes to soil. Remember the critter's poop along the Amazon River? This is the remaining 4 percent. It can be worm castings, chicken manure, or rabbit poop but it's a substance that's gone through an animal's body and come out on the other side. It's that little bit of "extra" that will help your kitchen garden be extra productive. Make sure any manure products you use are well aged (meaning at least one year old), or that they've been fully composted. You can also get bags of processed and dehydrated cow manure at your local garden center. Fresh manure contains various pathogens, so look for composted or processed manures instead.

Is 103 the most perfect ever soil blend? Not sure. Is 103 a simple way that anyone can make their own soil blend without mining peat bogs or figuring out what the things ending in -lite do? I think so. 103 works, very well, and it's as simple and natural as I can get it while still creating a blend that provides great growth in the garden. Are there lots of other things you can add to your soil beyond the 103? Of course! But to start, just grab these three components, plus the bonus 4 percent.

And, just so you know, every garden pictured in this book was grown with this soil blend—no synthetic fertilizers, no peat moss or vermiculite; just the 103. So if you don't believe me when I say that 103 works, ask the gardens.

Amend Your Own Soil

If you'd prefer to dig and amend your existing soil rather than create a blend from scratch, here are a few guidelines to make that possible.

If your soil is mostly clay, use about 25 percent of your soil and add 25 percent sand and 50 percent compost and then an additional 3 to 4 percent of well-aged manure or worm castings. In other words, every time you put in one shovel of your clay soil, you'll also put in one shovel of sand, and two shovels of compost, and then just a cup or two of castings or manure.

If you've got mostly sandy soil, you'll mix 33 percent of your soil, 33 percent topsoil, and 33 percent compost and then the bonus castings, too. For every shovel of compost, you'll also have a shovel of sandy soil, and then a bit more castings or manure.

If you have your own compost and would like to begin that way, add one part sand to one part compost to one part topsoil, and then also add a little of—you guessed it—castings or manure.

Finally, if you have a dark soil and mostly silt, mix one part of your soil with equal parts sand and compost (you may need to find some clay to dig up, too, if your soil is lacking structure).

Fill the Garden

Now that you know how to mix the best soil for your kitchen garden, how do you get this mix into your garden? You'll do this either with individual bags of soil, sand, and compost or with a bulk truck delivery. Bags can be great for convenience and small projects but the higher costs and the plastic wrapping

(be sure to reuse your bags!) are a bummer. Trucks are wonderful for getting large amounts of soil to your garden at a much lower price, but the mess and the shoveling can be tough (luckily, you only have to do this part once).

To decide whether you should buy bags or order a truck, we've got to do more math together. Don't worry: This time, the math adds up correctly.

Return to the measurements you decided upon for your raised beds. To determine the amount of soil you'll need, calculate the cubic feet of each bed and add them.

In case you forgot, the cubic foot measurement of each bed is found by multiplying length x width x height. And, if you have multiple beds of different sizes, calculate this for each bed and add them for the total.

For my kitchen garden, the beds are 7 feet (2.1 m) long, 2½ feet (0.8 m) wide, and 2 feet (0.6 m) tall. As a result, each bed's cubic feet is 7 x 2.5 x 2 (2.1 x 0.8 x 0.6 m), which equals 35 cubic feet (1 cubic m) each. And I have six gardens, so that means the total cubic feet of the garden area is 210.

DETERMINE FILL AMOUNTS

Multiply to determine the cubic feet of your kitchen garden.

1. Measure the length, width, and height of the gardens.

2. Multiply length x width x height to get cubic feet (cubic m) of each bed.

3. Add the cubic feet of multiple beds to get the total cubic feet (cubic m).

4. Divide that number by 27 to get the total number of cubic yards.

If you're building several gardens, as you start to add the cubic measurement of them, you'll eventually reach a value that merits a truck delivery. In the United States, 27 cubic feet equal 1 cubic yard. And, generally speaking, a nursery will send a delivery truck if you're ordering at least 2 cubic yards of soil.

Once you do the math for the cubic footage of your kitchen garden, you'll know whether you need a few bags or an entire dump truck's worth of soil. If you have a truck or a friend

with a truck (the best scenario, in my opinion), ask the soil yard if they'll fill you up with one-third coarse sand, one-third compost, and one-third topsoil—and you're set.

Generally, if you have a smaller garden that measures less than 25 cubic feet, you can fill your garden with bags purchased from your nursery. The bags of compost and sand from the hardware store or nursery are going to be in 1- to 3-cubic-foot quantities so buy the right amount of each type to equal your 103 needs.

A word to the wise: Each yard of material weighs about 1,000 pounds (453.5 kg). So, if you're filling the beds yourself, skip the gym on garden install day, invite a friend over, or call my kids and give them work to do!

To fill the beds, I prefer using a snow shovel because it enables you to get the most soil at once and lays against the edge of the garden easily as you place it into the box. To protect your garden bed, cover the edge with a weed barrier cloth to keep the shovels or the soil from marring the beds you've worked so hard to create.

As you start to fill the beds, it's a good idea to water in the soil. The sand and compost soil blend can be quite fluffy and the water will help the soil settle a bit, enabling you to fill the beds to the top. Once they are filled to the top, you've officially completed the dirtiest work of the garden process.

To keep your soil and plants healthy, add compost regularly, as well as more of the 4 percent, whenever you suspect your plants need it. I also recommend getting a soil test every few years to ensure your plants have all the nutrition they need. Soil test kits are available through most cooperative extension services at your state's land-grand university. You can also purchase them from independent soil testing laboratories online.

There are also DIY soil test kits available and I do, in fact, have one and I have used it, but I have to say I never know how accurate it is. Testing with a DIY soil test kit has mixed results. Though the news may come too late in some cases, I often find that the plants tell me more about the state of my soil (by not producing, by being too green, or by just sitting there) than the kit does.

Laboratory soil tests are much more accurate. This kind of official test won't tell you everything about your entire garden, but it will be able to tell you what nutrients are there and which are lacking. So, if you're having serious issues with your garden, or it's just not performing as you'd hoped (and I hope that's not the case), call in the experts to tell you what's up.

Though I can't recommend all the soil test kits with confidence, I can confidently say that compost can cure just about anything.

In fact, I have another mantra for it: When in doubt, add more compost.

If you doubt your soil's health and wonder what to do about it, adding a few inches of compost is never a bad idea. And as you fall in love with compost, as a gardener is likely to do, you can even create your own. Learn about compost from me and the Gardenary garden coaches at gardenary.com/book.

Water

"You'll do your clients a huge favor if you can plan a watering solution for them from the very beginning.'"

I was just starting Rooted Garden and making plans for a DIY kit for my first clients and talking with a raised garden provider who was kind enough to coach me on what might make my clients and, in turn, my business, succeed.

"You rarely think about water at the beginning but, then, somewhere in the middle, the presence or absence of a consistent watering plan is what makes or breaks the garden."

He was right.

For my first few clients, I delivered a raised bed, soil bags, plants, and seeds. But the watering was all on them.

Within a few months, after seeing some of their struggling plants, I learned my lesson: There has to be an upfront plan for watering or it just won't happen. From then on, every garden design came with a plan for irrigation, too. Even if our client had no formal irrigation in place, we planned for the water system to be as automated as possible.

As you plan your soil mix and installation for your garden, plan the water installation, too. Water is, of course, an essential part of the kitchen garden setup and, even though nothing needs to be watered at this moment, this is the time to plan for how the H_2O will, eventually, flow to your plants.

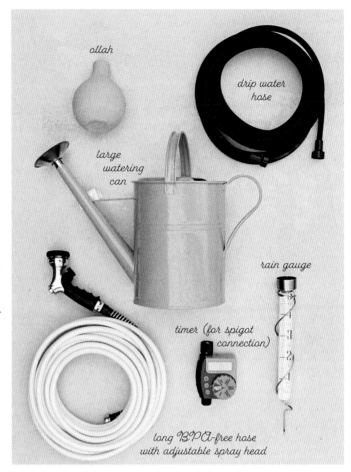

ollah

drip water hose

large watering can

rain gauge

timer (for spigot connection)

long BPA-free hose with adjustable spray head

Let's think about when, how, and from what source you'll water your kitchen garden. Kitchen garden plants love consistent water that's as close to rainwater as possible.

Most kitchen garden plants need about 1 inch (2.5 cm) of water per week—depending on the evaporation rate. And, your garden doesn't just need 1 inch (2.5 cm) of water; it needs it consistently.

Consistency is the key with watering. Plants are a lot like people: they thrive with a reliable routine (and they stress otherwise). When you water your plants on a schedule, their growth excels. I'm no psychiatrist and I've never done any plant counseling, but I'm 100 percent certain plants grow better for people they can depend on.

Just as with soil, the goal with watering your garden is to think about nature. In fact, nature's water is about as perfect as you can get. The more you can get rainwater on your garden, the better. Rainwater is more than just water; it has dissolved minerals that feed your plants, providing benefits well beyond the moisture it gives. And, unlike tap water, rainwater hasn't been treated with chlorine or other additives that can negatively affect your vegetable plants.

Ways to Water

Even as you plan for manually irrigating your kitchen garden, know you'll also be tracking the rainfall and using as much rainwater as possible.

Beyond doing a rain dance, there are a few other ways you can get consistent water to your kitchen garden. You can water by hand with a hose or watering can, with a spigot connection, or with a formal irrigation system.

Each system has its benefits and challenges, so it's important to choose the method that works best for you and stay flexible to alter your system if needed.

Hand Watering

The benefit of watering by hand is you're less likely to waste water. Because it's a chore, you likely won't do it unless necessary. This is, honestly, the best way to conserve water in the garden. But the challenge with hand watering is that it won't be as consistent for your plants and you'll be more than likely to stress your plants at some point by forgetting to water or delaying watering too long.

To be most effective, hand water in the early mornings, as this gives your plants plenty of time to dry out throughout the day. Focus on watering the roots, not the leaves, and use a spray attachment that enables a soft spray (think about imitating raindrops) rather than a hard and forceful one.

Spigot Connection

Connecting a timer and drip hose to your spigot is the closest you can get to automation without having a formal irrigation system. It's a great way to give your plants a consistent watering schedule and the timer is easy to adjust, as needed. Drip irrigation kits are available at most hardware stores.

Because you'll be taking over the spigot with this attachment, it's smart to use a Y-connector on the spigot so you can continue to use the water line for other things beyond the garden. After attaching the Y-connector, apply a battery-operated timer. To the timer, attach a pressure regulator that ensures not too much pressure comes out into the drip lines at once. Finally, you'll attach a PVC or poly tubing (with no holes) that will carry the water from the spigot to the garden.

Once your line has reached the garden area, pull a PVC or poly tube up into each garden, being sure each is securely connected to the source. Cover the installed line with soil, then add an elbow bracket and attach drip tubing on top of your soil bed.

If you want your irrigation lines hidden under your garden beds (and most of our clients do), the time to choose your irrigation method is before you install the gravel in your garden area. If you choose to use the spigot connection or the formal irrigation method, digging trenches for your water lines is essential before covering the garden area with gravel.

Track rainfall and capture as much rainwater as possible

Hand water as necessary

Create a spigot connection to run water to your garden as needed

Use a formal irrigation system with drip tubing or low spray heads

A trench that's about 4 to 6 inches (10.2 to 15.2 cm) deep will protect your irrigation tubing from any digging or impact that occurs and allow you to bring irrigation into the garden bed easily.

Even though creating a spigot connection and using a formal irrigation system are both possible to do yourself, it's fine to hire an irrigationist or landscaper to do this work for you. With Rooted Garden, finding certified irrigationists was an important investment for me. When it comes to digging trenches and connecting to clients' water systems, I wanted to be sure we were doing it in the very best way.

Formal Irrigation

A formal irrigation system is one in which all lines are tied to the home's vacuum breaker and a timer is connected to the lines that turns the water on and off at specific times and intervals during the week. This is a foolproof way to ensure water gets consistently to all parts of your garden, but it is a significant expense. If you do choose this option, it's best to purchase a rain sensor that connects with your timer that turns off your system when there's been plenty of rain on the garden.

Speaking of rain, collecting as much rain as possible, no matter the method you use for irrigating, is a wise choice. Even if you don't have a formal rain barrel, simply cutting off a gutter and having it deliver rainwater into a large bucket to be used later means using more of what's natural and limiting your home's water usage. With the rain you collect, you can fill watering cans.

Water Maintenance

It's happened more than a few times: Our client calls to tell us their garden isn't looking good. We head out to see what's happening and they're right—things don't look good. Plants are scorched. Soil is parched. So, we head back to the irrigation panel. Guess what? It's off. Completely off. Or, it's set to the schedule that worked six months ago, but not now.

It's important to monitor both the rain and temperature changes each month in the garden. A rain gauge is an excellent way to know how much has fallen each week. And by knowing the temperature, you can better gauge how quickly the water is going to evaporate.

Wind, humidity, and temperature all play a role in how fast your garden's water evaporates. Without sounding too much like a meteorologist, let me just sum things up to say you need to check on your garden regularly, especially when the weather is hot.

Taking note of rainfall and how quickly it evaporates helps you know when to turn off your automatic irrigation system or crank it up. Increase your water at the height of sun and temperature levels and decrease it when temperatures fall in the cooler parts of the growing season.

Beyond tracking rainfall and temperature, check the timer to be sure the battery is working and, if you have one, check the formal irrigation system to be sure it's ON. If you have an electronic system running, it's a good idea to turn it on while you're out tending and watch the system run through a full cycle. This allows you to check for leaks, see what may be getting too much or too little water, and ensure that things are working as they should.

But, here's something to remember: The answer isn't always more water. I've noticed a lot of new gardeners often see a problem in the garden and immediately think, "Quick, the garden needs water!"

Although more water may be the answer, it isn't THE answer for every garden problem. Before you add more water, be certain it's necessary. Here are some signs of water trouble in your garden:

» The garden's surface is dry and cracked

» You see wilted or brown leaves

» Some leaves are turning yellow, mildewing, or rotting

These are all signs that your water needs adjusting. The first two indicate not enough water. The latter may indicate too much water.

Summary

Even though your 103 blend is 103 percent perfect and your watering system is on point, there's a key word I need you to remember: change.

That's what happens every single day in the kitchen garden. I'm sorry to say that even though your new garden started close to perfect, that doesn't mean it will stay that way. Every single minute the soil and water level are changing. On the upside, nutrients and moisture are moving to the roots of your plants. On the downside, there's not an endless supply of those things. You can count on it: your garden will be counting on you for help—this is what makes you a "gardener" after all.

I think someone somewhere said that the only thing that's certain is change and it's certainly true in the kitchen garden. Begin with certainty that this simple soil mix and your preferred watering system are going to work in your garden. But don't assume it will stay perfect.

Take care of the soil and water and your garden will, for the most part, take care of your plants. Don't let those bags of fertilizer and other garden products at the hardware store (and the accompanying claims of supernatural growth) overwhelm you. Remember that little tomato vine thriving on the banks of the Amazon hundreds of years ago. Think about nature, give it a little help, and you'll be picking cherry tomatoes in no time.

Speaking of cherry tomatoes, I think it's about time we start planting this kitchen garden, don't you? Well, don't just stand there with the water hose, let's dig in to Part Two.

PART TWO

GROWING IN THE KITCHEN GARDEN

CHAPTER FIVE

PLAN

Create Your Kitchen Garden Calendar

• • • • • •

Repeat after me: "I will not go to the plant store until I have a plan." Say it again. I promise I'm making this pledge right alongside you. Too many times, my first instinct in starting my garden was to buy plants—and it didn't go well.

There is a form of shopping you *should* do before planting your garden though—at the farmers' market. One of the best ways to plan your priorities for your kitchen garden is to regularly visit a farmers' market or join a local CSA for a few seasons. (Warning: Once you start, your taste buds won't let you stop).

Although I may be able to help you set up and start planting your kitchen garden, it's your local farmer who really knows the specifics of your particular seasons, how to get the timing right, and how to make the most of your climate.

When I move to a new town (and I seem to do that a lot), the farmers' market is the first place I visit. Local farmers are a wealth of information. If the farmer has beans, lean in and kindly say, "Wow, these beans look great. When did you plant them? "Or, if she has the best-looking tomatoes, ask, "When did you plant these? They look amazing."

Snag a quick photo each week to document what's on the farmers' tables. Before you know it, you'll have created your planting calendar. If you see something on the table, you know it was planted just two or three months earlier, depending on its size and maturity.

To me, farmers' markets, CSAs, and kitchen gardens go hand in hand. Although you'll get to enjoy a lot from your garden, there will still be fruits and vegetables you'll need to buy to fill your plate each day. As you start to taste what local and seasonal food is like, you'll be more willing to take a special trip and support your local farmer.

After shopping with the farmers, not at the plant store, it's time to make a planting plan.

Although plants may all look similar when all lined up in their 4-inch (10.2 cm) pots or nursery flats, there are distinct categories each plant belongs in—some similar and some vastly different from their neighbor on the garden center bench.

In this chapter, I'll teach you my special process for categorizing plants and matching them with your garden's seasons. Because I've gardened in so many different places and used so many different plants, I needed a system I could apply anywhere, in any space. And, so, over the years I developed this one.

By categorizing plants, particularly kitchen garden plants, you'll be able to make sense of information previously reserved for supposed "green thumbs" and make a plan that will work for you.

Plants can be categorized based on their *season*, *size*, *lifespan*, and *productivity*. And all this is closely tied to the family to which each plant belongs.

The good news is, there are so many plants. The better news is, there's a way, even for a brand-new gardener, to simplify and understand each plant's unique characteristics and its possibilities in the kitchen garden.

Getting to Know Your Climate

Before we set up our plant categories, let's take a minute to get to know your climate a little better. Though you may have lived in your current space for a few months, years, or, perhaps, your whole life, you may never have noticed each month as you're about to.

Picture your kitchen garden as a guesthouse for plants. Each guest has particular needs and wants—this much space to spread out, this much time to stay, and needs the temperature to be just so. Plant guests can be like my kids: picky.

By learning your climate's temperature, rainfall, and sunlight measurements for each month, you'll know best which guests can stay each month and for how long. Consider this step as the booking calendar for your garden: deciding which plants are welcome to stay and which ones just might not be made for your guesthouse.

Lots of gardening experts will tell you to, first, learn your garden "zone," before planting. But, honestly, garden zones are much too general to inform you of what's technically possible in the unique space you've created. I've gardened in so many different climates and what the books say I can do in a particular zone and what I experience in my garden are often two very different things. Plus, gardening zones specify a first and last frost date as the most significant times of the year, leading new gardeners to believe they can only grow between those two days. In truth, the only information the frost date reveals is when the cool season ends and the warm season begins (more on these two seasons in a second).

There's so much more to the kitchen garden than zones and frost dates. This is why, over the years, I developed my kitchen garden seasons system. The best way to know what's possible in your unique garden is to know your garden's seasons and the best way to know your seasons is to understand the general weather for each month of the year. This exercise is so much more detailed than a "zone" number and will be more specific and helpful to your unique location.

If you haven't already, grab your Garden Journal download at gardenary.com/book and fill in the average high temperature, low temperature, sunlight hours, and rainfall amounts for each month in your hometown. These numbers will help you identify which general season you're in each month of the year. You can also use the chart below to track this information.

CLIMATE CHART

Name of Town/Longitude and Latitude: _____

Month	Average High Temp	Average Low Temp	Average Sunlight Hours	Average Rainfall Amount
January				
February				
March				
April				
May				
June				
July				
August				
September				
October				
November				
December				

Once you've filled in this information, you can, generally, place each month into a particular season. Not every garden will have every season, and some may just have two.

Refer to these temperature ranges to label each month in your garden according to its season.

COLD/OFF SEASON has an average high temperature of about 30°F (-1°C), or lower, with a guaranteed chance of frost or snow.

COOL SEASON has an average high temperature between 35°F and 65°F (1.6°C and 18.3°C) with a likely chance of frost or snow.

WARM SEASON has an average high temperature between 65°F and 85°F (18.3°C and 29.4 °C) with no chance of frost.

HOT SEASON has an average high temperature that's 85°F (29.4°C) or higher and no chance of anything close to cold.

SEASONS CHART

Month	Season
January	
February	
March	
April	
May	
June	
July	
August	
September	
October	
November	
December	

Not every month falls exactly into the same season all month long; some months can be split between two seasons, but you get the idea.

Unless you live in the Arctic or on the Equator, every town or city, no matter the climate, has an arc to its seasons. There's the coolest period and the warmest period and then usually two periods in between those more extreme seasons.

For instance, in Houston, there's a long cool season (the coldest time, if you can call it that), then a warm season, then a hot season (the warmest), and then another warm season. Repeat.

And in Chicago, there's a long cold season (very, very cold), a cool season, a warm season, and then another cool season. And, repeat.

Most other climates have this same arc: coldest, warmer, warmest, back to warmer, and then back to coldest.

It's the two in-between seasons most gardeners miss. In fact, the gardening resources I first studied led me to believe I could only garden in that warmest season of the year. While the majority of growing can certainly happen during that period, there is lots of growing that can happen on either side of it, too, especially those "in-between" seasons. In Houston's case, the two warm seasons and, in Chicago's case, the two cool seasons. More growing seasons means more time to grow and I like the sound of that, don't you?

Even without some type of insulating cover or a greenhouse, there are some things that will continue to grow below ground during the cold season. But, for the purpose of this chapter, we will mostly focus on the cool, warm, and hot seasons in the garden with the understanding you can stretch the cool season into the cold season with protective frost cloths, greenhouses, cold frames, and covers if—and when—you're ready.

Now that you understand your kitchen garden seasons, it's time to understand the plants. Each plant has a unique season of growth, and a relatively consistent size, duration, and possible production level. Each of these characteristics ends up being quite similar to other plants found in the same plant family. As a result, families are the primary way we categorize plants.

Plant Families

When I started gardening and eagerly approached the seed rack at the local nursery, my excitement quickly turned to overwhelm. Beans and corn, tomatoes, watermelon, peppers, squash, cabbage, arugula. And that was just the first row. Each packet felt like an entirely different species and a unique garden mystery I'd need to solve before calling myself a "gardener."

Were there a thousand different plants here?

There may, in fact, be thousands of edible plants in the world. But the good news is, those thousands of plants can be divided into a relatively small amount of plant families or groups.

Plant families are a lot like people families. Although every family member isn't exactly alike, there are common traits that make getting to know each of them a little simpler. Just like family members usually speak the same language, enjoy similar food, and have some common physical characteristics, plant family members often require similar care, thrive in the same temperatures, and grow to a similar size. There are always outliers, but the dominant traits keep showing up.

The genetic codes of family similarities are good news when you're trying to feel less awkward around your second cousin—and for kitchen gardeners like me and you.

Once you understand a little about one member of a plant family, chances are, you'll likely know more about that plant's family members, too. And don't worry. There aren't a thousand edible plant families in the world. In fact, most of the foods you and I enjoy in our everyday meals fit into fewer than fifteen plant families. And in the common kitchen garden, you'll likely only grow five to eight plant families.

Eight or even fifteen is a much easier number than 1000, don't you agree?

So, forget the seed rack for a moment and just meet some kitchen garden plant families.

Apiaceae

First, the Apiaceae family, also known as the umbellifer, or carrot family. Carrots, as you likely already know, have long narrow roots and tall green stems with feathery leaves. Other members of the umbellifer family include celery, cilantro, dill, fennel, parsley, and parsnip. Nearly all these family members enjoy living in the same home as the carrot: the cool season, growing in loose sandy soil, and receiving consistent water. The seeds for each of these plants look similar, too, and the growing time for all these plants is about the same: at least 60 days from seed. I like to call Apiaceae plants "medium" plants. They don't take too terribly long to grow and don't require too much space—just a happy medium kind of plant.

Besides fennel, most Apiaceae plants don't need much space in the garden but work well if planted in rows or blocks. All can be started by seed planted directly into the garden (many won't transplant well) and will be planted in your kitchen garden early in the cool season. From thinning to harvesting, there's a little more tending that goes into caring for your umbellifer plants. Once established, these plants can, mostly, care for themselves during the majority of their growing period. If you need a kitchen garden plant that grows over a few months requiring little more than water, the umbellifer family is one to meet.

Asteraceae

Next up is the Asteraceae family, also called the aster or daisy family.

You may recognize the word, "aster" from the popular fall flower. But the aster family includes hundreds of varieties of lettuces and greens commonly eaten as salads. Greens like romaine lettuce, iceberg lettuce, radicchio, endive, and more, are all in this family. Asters also include dandelions and sunflowers.

Buttercrunch lettuce, one of the most well-known aster family members, love the cool season and is a small and short-season plant. Unlike the carrot, buttercrunch has a very small root structure and can be planted in a fairly shallow box (just 6 inches [15.2 cm] deep). Buttercrunch and its fellow lettuce varieties grow well from seed planted directly into the garden and will continue to produce new leaves from their centers until the weather warms above 80°F (26.6°C). At that point, lettuces produce a tall center flower stalk (called bolting) and, eventually, develop seeds that can be saved for next season's plants.

Aster family plants are some of the easiest to grow in a kitchen garden as you can fit so many in a small space, the same plants give you continuous harvests, and the smaller plants require less tending. If you're looking for a plant family to start with in your kitchen garden, this is it.

Amaranthaceae

Want "super foods" in your kitchen garden? Meet the Amaranthaceae family. Also known as the goosefoot family, the amaranth family includes beets, spinach, Swiss chard, and quinoa. These plants provide loads of vitamins K and A (and plenty of others) and have a unique betalain pigment (the red you see in roots and stems), which has antioxidant and anti-inflammatory components.

Most of this family enjoys growing in cooler temperatures, but Swiss chard is a biennial that lives for two years in the garden if temperatures aren't too extreme. Though beets only provide one root harvest per plant, you can harvest the greens again and again, just as you can with Swiss chard and spinach. If I were to rank this family in terms of growing difficulty, I'd begin with Swiss chard, then try spinach, then beets, and finally quinoa.

In my experience, this plant family does best when started from seed planted directly into the garden, but Swiss chard and spinach can be started indoors or with a transplant from a nursery.

Plants in this family are either categorized as small and short or medium-size plants.

Cucurbitaceae

When you're ready to test your gardening skills, it's time to grow Cucurbitaceae, or the cucumber family. The plants in this family are some I can't get enough of like cucumber and watermelon. These plants do best when planted by seed sown directly into the garden. And, they need quite warm weather before they're ready to take off. There's no doubt—these are warm-season plants.

Many plants in this family either need a trellis to grow on or a large spot in the garden. Summer squash and zucchini both grow into large plants, whereas the long vines of cucumber and winter squash grow up a trellis or along the ground for what seems like forever. These plants love a consistent amount of water and are prone to diseases and pests, such as powdery mildew and squash vine borer.

In other words, buyer beware. There's a bit of a challenge to growing these crops, but the payoff is delicious. When you're standing in the garden pathway with cucumber juice dripping down your chin, you'll know you've arrived in kitchen garden heaven.

Solanaceae

If you've seen a garden photo, you've almost certainly seen a picture of this family. The quintessential kitchen garden harvest always includes loads of tomatoes—for good reason. They are the crowning jewel for the kitchen gardener. Tomatoes are part of the Solanaceae family, which also includes eggplant, peppers, potatoes, and tomatillos.

These plants love to grow in warm to hot temperatures and receive loads of sunshine. They have deep roots, so they prefer a bigger garden. Nearly all need support.

Plants in this family are hungry for loads of nutrients. They'll take whatever your soil gives them—and then they'll want more and then some more, thank you. Most are also in need of pruning and weekly care during their growing season. So, don't plant these veggies just before you head out of town for three months.

But, no matter how much work they require, members of this family make it well worth your while.

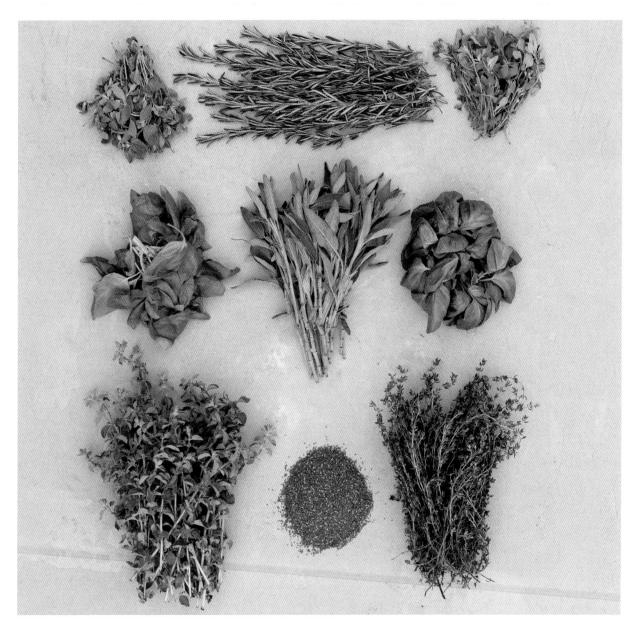

Lamiaceae

The very best family to begin with in the kitchen garden is the Lamiaceae family, the mint family. If grown in the right conditions, these plants can provide herbs that grow and produce for months and months. Kitchen garden plants in this family include basil, lemon balm, oregano, rosemary, and sage. This plant family originated in the Mediterranean region—think sand, sun, and heat when planting most members of this family.

Most of the Lamiaceae herbs are difficult to start from seed but grow well from transplants and cuttings. When you're ready to grow them, buy small organic herb plants and divide them, or start a few cuttings once they've matured a bit.

Brassicaceae

Also known as the mustard family, Brassicaceae includes arugula, broccoli, cabbage, kale, radish, and, of course, mustard. Sometimes called cole crops or brassicas, this family's plants are packed with vitamins. Except for radishes and arugula, most Brassicaceae plants need at least 1 square foot (0.09 m²) to spread out and show off.

Most Brassicaceae enjoy being planted in the cooler parts of the season. In fact, broccoli, cauliflower, and kale can all be planted well before the last spring frost. And their leaves are able to stand up against moderate frosts and cold temperatures.

Although it's amazing to watch broccoli, cauliflower, and Brussels sprouts grow from seed to flower bud, plant these with caution in your kitchen garden—mostly due to their size and time needs. It may take a broccoli plant nearly 2 to 3 square feet (0.18 to 0.27 m²) to reach full size and more than 3 months to produce a flower bud I can harvest. But, from the same size spot, I can harvest at least 10 pounds (4.5 kg) of kale all season long.

Fabaceae

Perhaps the simplest first step in a kitchen garden is planting a bean seed. It's so easy to handle, quite simple to plant, and, in just a few days, it pops its head out of the soil!

The Fabaceae family, also known as the pea and bean family, is a great one for the kitchen garden. Otherwise known as legumes, plants in this family are easy to grow. In general, shell, sugar, and snow peas grow in cooler months and can be planted several months before the last frost, whereas most types of beans, including green, lima, snap, and the many types of dried beans, enjoy warmer temperatures.

I recommend planting all your legumes from seed rather than as transplants.

As we all work toward a more plant-based diet, harvests from the Fabaceae family make that possible to do from your kitchen garden. With peas in the cool season, beans in the warm, and dried beans and peas kept for winter, there's lots of potential to go garden to table with this plant family nearly all year long.

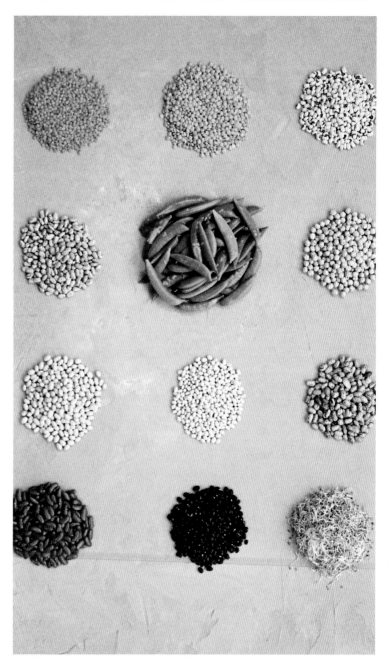

Amaryllidaceae

Perhaps better summarized as the onion or allium family, Amaryllidaceae includes chives, garlic, leeks, and onions, and, at one time, also included asparagus (now in its own unique family).

Most Amaryllidaceae family members grow from bulbs. Some can be planted underground before the weather turns cold (I'm talking to you, garlic), whereas others are best planted in spring (hello, onions).

The very first edible plant I learned to grow was chives, introduced when my mom came to visit and left a terra cotta pot full of garlic chives on the front step. I gave very little care to the pot but was cutting chives every week for omelets and soups. Though I felt nothing but chaos with four kids under four, the feeling I experienced when I cut a few chives before breakfast was one I couldn't get enough of. If you want to start simply with a single plant in a container, one from the allium family may get you off to a great start.

OTHER PLANT FAMILIES *for the* KITCHEN GARDEN

Family Name	Common Name	Plants	Additional Info
Convolvulaceae	morning glory family	sweet potato	staple crop in the south; does best in summer's heat; potatoes harvested in fall
Gramineae	grass family	corn, lemongrass, millet	requires a lot of space so often best grown outside the kitchen garden
Lauraceae	laurel family	avocado, bay laurel, cinnamon	not cold tolerant; bay laurel is a woody herb great for pots; great for climates with no frost
Malvaceae	hibiscus family	cotton, okra, roselle	thrives in heat; give plants plenty of room
Polygonaceae	buckwheat family	rhubarb	perennial; cold-tolerant; stalks are harvested in spring
Rosaceae	rose family	apples, peaches, pears, raspberries, strawberries, etc.	perennial and/or woody; can handle cold winter temperatures; best planted near kitchen gardens but not in them
Rutaceae	rue or citrus family	grapefruits, kumquats, lemons, limes, orange, etc.	tropical; not frost tolerant; best grown in pots
Zingiberaceae	ginger family	cardamom, ginger, turmeric	produce underground rhizomes that are dried and ground for spice; tropical plants; do best in containers; not frost tolerant but perennial

Each season has its own set of plants that will be large and lengthy in growth and others that will be small and short. I've found that, generally speaking, a plant's size predicts its length of time until harvest. A large plant needs about 1 square foot (0.09 m²) of space and about 75 to 90 days before harvest. Small plants take up a fraction of that space in the garden and take 25 to 45 days before harvest. For instance, in the cool season, radishes are small and ready to harvest in about 45 days, whereas broccoli is large and needs 75 to 90 days before its ready for harvest.

For the **COOL, WARM,** and **HOT SEASONS,** there are a number of plant families that will happily make a home in your garden and stay for a while.

In the **COLD SEASON,** when temperatures are below freezing to just over 40°F (4.4°C), the large and lengthy plants include asparagus, garlic, onion, and rhubarb.

For the **COOL SEASON,** when temperatures range from 35°F to 65°F (1.6°C to 18.3° C), the small and short plants include lettuces, radishes, and other greens. The large and lengthy plants include broccoli, cabbage, peas, and other brassicas.

In the **WARM SEASON,** when temperatures range from 65°F to 85°F (18.3°C to 29.4°C), the small and short plants include basil and bush beans and the large and lengthy plants include cucumbers, squash, tomatoes, and zucchini.

In the **HOT SEASON,** when temperatures range from 70°F to over 90°F (21°C to 32°C), the small and short plants include basil and all woody herbs, and the large and lengthy plants include eggplants, okra, and tomatillos.

PLANT CLASSIFICATION CHART

Season	Family	Size	Duration (Days)
Cool	Asteraceae	Small	30 to 45
Cool	Apiaceae	Small to Medium	45 to 60
Cool	Brassicaceae	Medium to Large	60 to 90
Cool	Fabaceae	Medium to Large	60 to 75
Cool	Amaryllidaceae	Small	60 to 120
Cool	Amaranthaceae	Medium	45 to 90
Cool	Polygonaceae	Large	60
Warm	Solanaceae	Large	60 to 90
Warm	Cucurbitaceae	Large	60 to 90
Warm	Fabaceae	Medium to Large	60 to 75
Warm	Lamiaceae	Medium	30 to 75
Hot	Gramineae	Large	70 to 90
Hot	Convolvulaceae	Large	75 to 90+
Hot	Malvaceae	Large	60 to 90
Hot	Zingiberaceae	Large	60 to 120

COLD SEASON plant families either lie dormant underground during the cold season or continue to grow slowly through the coolest seasons in milder climates. Dormant crops include garlic, onions, rhubarb, and asparagus. Spinach and other greens grow slowly.

COOL SEASON plant families are Apiaceae, Amaranthaceae, Asteraceae, Brassicaceae, and Fabaceae. Essentially, it's time to grow lettuces and greens, root crops, and peas.

WARM SEASON

plant families are some Asteraceae, Cucurbitaceae, Fabaceae, and Solanaceae. These crops are, what we consider, a "quintessential kitchen garden harvest"— beans, cucumbers, squash, tomatoes, and zucchini.

HOT SEASON crops

are better known in tropical and subtropical climates and include some Solanaceae plants such as eggplant and tomatillo; as well as lesser known families such as Convolvulaceae and Malvaceae plants such as sweet potato and okra.

Once you know which season each plant grows in, the next step is to know their size and duration—basically, how long they'll need to grow in the garden and how big they'll become. Generally speaking, plants that tend to be smaller take a shorter time to be ready to harvest and the opposite is true for larger plants. They grow big and tall or grow lengthy vines and take more time to mature.

Prioritize Kitchen Garden Plants

It's time to prioritize and select a specific number of each type of plants to invite as guests into your garden each season of the year based on your food preferences, garden space, and how long you're willing to wait for the harvest.

I always feel badly when a client who's selected a small kitchen garden then sends us a list of all the things they'd like planted—tomatoes, squash, zucchini, beans, and eggplant. It's fun to know they'd like to grow all those things but also such a bummer to break the news that we can only fit a few of those large plants in their small bed.

So what's your priority?

Kitchen gardens can be developed for all sorts of reasons—pleasure, production, experimentation, or just for beauty. I have one chef client who prioritizes edible flowers for her culinary creations. Another loves the beauty of her cottage garden and enjoys letting some plants continue to grow without harvest just for the aesthetic. And another would make a dish each night from her kitchen garden, if possible.

That's one of the best things about a kitchen garden—you can create it to meet your preferences. If regular production is your goal, plant as many small and short plants as possible. If getting lots of one particular vegetable from the garden is the goal, then make room to ensure that plant gets as much space, time, and attention as your garden can afford it.

In each season, you can grow six to twelve of each small plant per square foot (0.09 m²), four to six medium plants per square foot (0.09 m²), and about one large and lengthy plant per square foot (0.09 m²). For every square foot (0.09 m²) in the garden, you'll either choose one large and lengthy plant, or from four to twelve small, short plants. Each season will have its own priorities but be sure to plant your favorites first.

Keep the small and short plants on the outside of your bed, put the medium plants in the middle, and place the large plants in the center. On a border garden, put large plants along the back of the garden, medium plants in the middle, and small plants toward the front.

Once you've prioritized your plants, begin to plan where you'll position them that season inside your kitchen garden based on their size.

Now let's make a planting plan for each season in your kitchen garden. You'll find out how to bring this plan to life in the next chapter.

In your kitchen garden journal, there's a space to list the large, medium, and small plants for each season and to note how much space you'll need to devote to each one, and how many plants you'll need to fill that space.

Make a plan for each season, realizing that your seasons may overlap a bit. For instance, your warm season plants may be finishing up when it's time to plant your hot season plants. And your hot season plants may not have fruited before it's time to plant cool season things. It's true—plans are made to be broken, at the very least flexed. But, having a plan really is the best way to start. You'll modify it throughout the year, but it gives you parameters to know where you're headed and keeps you from overbuying or underusing your space.

Season-by-Season Planting

COLD SEASON Most things in this season are lying dormant underground, unless they are under frost cover. In the cold season, you can plant Brassicas, Alliums, and some root crops.

COOL SEASON As much as sixty days before the last threat of frost, you can begin sowing seeds directly in the garden of cold-tolerant vegetables such as carrots and peas, and cole crops such as broccoli, cauliflower, and kale. Lettuces and any other plant that's moderately frost resistant can also be started indoors about thirty days before it's time to plant them in the garden.

WARM SEASON About thirty days before the warm season begins, it's time to start seeds for tomatoes and peppers indoors. You'll then move them into the garden as soon as the threat of frost has passed; after this point, you can plant seeds of squash, cucumber, and beans directly in the garden.

HOT SEASON If you have a hot season, those plants can be started thirty days before they should be moved out to the garden as well. These include eggplant, okra, and sweet potato.

SECOND COOL SEASON Toward the end of the hot season, or your warmest season, it's time to circle back to the plants you were growing before the heat arrived. Thirty days or so before the end of the hottest season, begin starting seeds indoors for the second cooler season, and then set them out into the garden as soon as the weather cools to the right temperature.

COLD SEASON BEGINS AGAIN After the second cooler season begins, in warmer climates, those plants will often continue to grow throughout the winter. In colder places, with frost and snow, it will be time to protect any cold-tolerant plants that can handle frosts with a cover or cold frame. For a longer harvest, include a few veggies that might be able to overwinter, such as root crops and greens, in your plan.

It's all this extra growing that makes the kitchen garden worth the investment. It's not just three months out of the year that you can be growing. In most cases, it's more like six or eight. In fact, I'll go so far as to say you can grow as much as ten months under the protection of a greenhouse, and all year long in temperate climates. The fun, literally, never stops growing.

Outside your kitchen garden boxes, note any trees, bushes, or pollinator-friendly plants you'd like to include around the perimeter. You can add native flowers that will welcome pollinators as well as blackberries, blueberries, and fruit trees that suit your climate.

Step-by-Step Kitchen Garden

As you plan your plants for the kitchen garden, keep in mind that the longer and larger your plants need to grow before harvest, the higher their level of difficulty. The sooner you can harvest from your plants in their life cycle, the greater your chances of success in the garden. If you're new to gardening, start with the easiest-to-grow crops, then progress to the more difficult ones.

If you'd like to keep things simple to start, or you want to ensure a continuous harvest, follow this course in your kitchen garden: first leaves, then roots, then fruit.

Begin by planting your kitchen garden primarily with plants that will be harvested for their leaves. As you master growing leaves, then plant vegetables that will be harvested for their roots. Finally, begin to grow those plants that are harvested for their fruit.

WOODY HERBS The simplest leaf harvest is from herbs, particularly the typical herbs we use in the kitchen for soups, dry rubs, and sauces. These include rosemary, oregano, thyme, and sage. If set up properly, you'll have success growing herbs from the very start. And the continuous harvests mean you'll push right past those expensive plastic cases of herbs at the grocery (a feeling that's only possible for a true kitchen gardener).

LETTUCE AND GREENS Beyond herbs, growing greens is the second simplest approach to kitchen garden plants. Just like herbs, lettuce leaves can be harvested repeatedly. You'll enjoy fresh salad cuts just a few weeks after planting, even from seed. From sweet lettuces to kale and Swiss chard, there are greens that can grow in your garden nearly year-round. The fact that most of these plants can be harvested numerous times means your kitchen garden will quickly begin to pay for its rent in your landscape.

ROOT CROPS After leaf harvests come root harvests, such as beets, carrots, and radishes, which follow in simplicity and production. Most root crops must be planted from seed and need to be thinned, so this adds a new level of difficulty. However, with the majority of your harvest underground and the plants needing little pruning or fertilization, growing roots is the next step in planting your kitchen garden. The wait will be longer than for greens and there's just one harvest per plant, but the result is more delicious than you can imagine.

FRUIT CROPS Plants such as tomatoes and cucumbers, grown for their fruit, are the most complicated and require the most patience. To reach the fruiting stage, these plants must grow from seed, develop deep roots, grow strong stems and leaves, produce flowers, and, then finally, fruit. These plants will need pruning and regular fertilizing and, even then, the fruit may be taken by pests or difficult weather. Nevertheless, a handful of cherry tomatoes or a basket of fresh cucumbers is a kitchen gardener's crown jewel and certainly worth the hard work.

If you're just beginning your kitchen garden, or you don't want one bit of disappointment, wait to grow fruiting plants until you have a few seasons of kitchen gardening behind you. Believe me, the endless harvests of herbs and greens are within your grasp in your very first season of kitchen gardening and even that will feel like a complete spoil.

I designed this area near a client's kitchen garden to include native flowers, fruit trees, bay laurel, and just for fun, some succulents.

QUICK TIPS *for* EASY HARVESTS

Woody Herbs [Lamiaceae Family]

›› Begin with locally grown plants

›› Harvest outside and lower leaves regularly within 2 weeks of planting

›› Water conservatively

Lettuce & Greens [Asteraceae Family]

›› Begin with seeds

›› Thin if necessary

›› Water consistently

›› Harvest outside and lower leaves frequently within 4 weeks of planting

Root Crops [Umbellifer, Brassica, and Amaranth Families]

›› Begin with seeds

›› Thin if necessary

›› Water consistently

›› Moderate fertilizer

›› Harvest a few at a time within 45 to 90 days after planting

Fruit Crops [Solanaceae and Cucurbit Families]

›› Begin with seeds or locally grown plants

›› Water deeply

›› Fertilize weekly or bi-weekly

›› Prune regularly

›› Protect, if necessary

›› Harvest 60 to 100 days after planting

Summary

If you've made it to the end of this chapter, you now have permission to go plant shopping. I know impulse purchases are so much more thrilling than making weather charts, but dead plants aren't thrilling at all.

Planning your kitchen garden based on your unique seasons connects you to your home and the seasonal changes throughout the year in a way nothing else can. Now that you understand the seasons and plant families, you're unstoppable in the kitchen garden. Speaking of unstoppable, you can't quit now. It's time to start planting.

CHAPTER SIX

PLANT

Begin to Grow in Your Kitchen Garden

● ● ● ● ● ●

I'm going to come right out and say it: You can pretty much ignore plant labels.

Because guess what? The plant tags in nurseries weren't created for kitchen gardeners. The plant tags tell you how far apart your plants should be if you're growing crops in long and wide rows on a farm or a large in-ground vegetable patch, not in your backyard's raised garden. So, when the tag says something like "space 3 to 4 feet apart (0.9 to 1.2 m) in 3-foot (0.9 m) rows," it's talking to the farmer who will have 40 or 60 feet (12.2 or 18.3 m) of each planting row with twenty or forty or more plants along the hill. Is this you? This isn't me. And this is not a kitchen garden.

Don't get me wrong: I'm so thankful we have farmers who farm in rows and plant lots and lots of food. We need more of them. This is, in no way, meant as disrespect to the farmers who plant in rows. Farmers: If any of you are reading this, please keep planting all the delicious things however you want and I will buy them all. And please don't hate me for breaking the plant spacing rules.

Just one look at my gardens and you'll know I like to pack in the plants. As in, please don't send the Proper Spacing Police my way, because I will certainly be brought in for questioning. I started planting my gardens this way after following all the plant tags' advice for spacing, like any proper new gardener would.

"Two to three feet apart?" Okay.

"Planted twelve inches apart in three-foot rows?" Yes sir.

I promise I was a very obedient gardener in the beginning. But a few months in, I regretted following the rules.

One: I got very little production out of my small space. Our first garden boxes were 4 feet by 4 feet (1.2 by 1.2 m), only about 16 square feet (1.48 m²) of total growing space. Following the plant tags' spacing guidelines, I had room for about four, maybe five tomato plants. And that was it. So, I'd waited all year for this one little box to grow something for

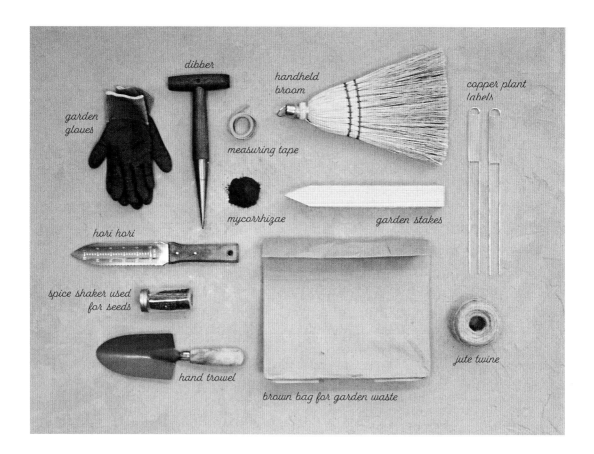

garden gloves

dibber

measuring tape

handheld broom

copper plant labels

mycorrhizae

garden stakes

hori hori

spice shaker used for seeds

hand trowel

brown bag for garden waste

jute twine

me and all I got were tomatoes. And if those failed or were stolen by the squirrels (which by the way, they were), I was devastated with no back up plan. Meanwhile, the tomatoes were very comfortable, lounging in their spacious luxury garden condo while I was left with an empty harvest basket and a bunch of plant tags.

Two: The bare soil was not my friend. When plants are spread way apart with nothing in between, there's a lot of soil left exposed to the elements. A lot. Bare soil dries out more quickly and is much more difficult to manage. When the soil was bare between my plants, I was constantly watering. Constantly. And on a hot, sunny day, I might have to water twice. (Did I mention I have four kids and a few other things to do besides hold a hose?) As much as I enjoyed my garden, I didn't love lugging a heavy hose around the garden beds in the summer heat twice a day.

Three: Things grew in those open spaces whether I planted them or not. After careful study, I can say with confidence that it's the weeds that write the plant tags. They know that if you put 2 or 3 feet (0.6 or 0.9 m) between your plants, they'll have way more sunlight and space to grow themselves—at least they did in my garden. After I was done wrangling the hose and keeping the bare soil watered for a few weeks, guess what happened? Things grew in those spaces. Grass, clover, and purslane—they weren't things I wanted to eat, and they were growing between the plants I wanted.

So, I thought to myself: "Self, if the bare soil is hard to manage and smaller plants seem to grow there anyway, why not plant smaller plants that you'd actually like to grow in that space? They'll protect the soil so you don't have to water so much; they'll keep you from having to pull weeds; and you might even get to harvest some extra things from your garden and not bank your entire season's success on those four tomato plants."

And myself said, "That is a very good idea."

I went with it. And guess what? It worked. Not perfectly, but as well or better than following the plant tag suggestions. It went so well I started doing this with our clients. It's called, "intensive planting"—a.k.a., packing in the plants.

If you've made it this far into the book, clearly you're a reader. But here's my advice: Don't read the plant tags. I mean, you can, if you want. But take the plant tag instruction as a mere suggestion, something to keep in mind. Not a rule or a law or a must.

Because we've created deep raised beds and we're gardening in a smaller space that will be tended more often, we can afford to plant our plants closer together, and more intensively. Which reminds me of another thing I like to say: Anything worth doing is worth doing intensively.

The idea behind intensive planting is that it will provide you with more harvests of more varieties more often. Sounds good right? It's great, but it's not for everyone.

INTENSIVE PLANTING PLEDGE

1. I will tend my garden weekly—maybe even several times per week.

2. I will prune my garden regularly and use the harvest as often as possible.

3. If some plants are getting crowded, I will remove the ones that aren't as important to me.

4. I will double check on my plants so they feel cared for, even though I have a lot of them in a small space.

5. I will be okay if not everything works out well because I got to try growing lots of things all in one season, which means I learned way more than I would have if I'd just grown a few rows of one or two things.

6. I will not be intimidated by rule followers who tell me I'm wrong for not following plant tag instructions.

7. I'll message Nicole when I harvest so much more than any of my rule-following friends (but will do my best to not to be too braggy).

Intensive planting does not work for people who don't tend their gardens. Why? Because intensive planting isn't a "set it and forget it" kind of garden. The generous spacing is for someone who will plant, water, fertilize, and harvest just one crop and call it a day.

But, the whole point of setting up the garden in the first place is to create a space for us to practice a new hobby, to be entertained, to learn something new, right? There's a reason "tended regularly" is in my definition of a "kitchen garden."

If you only have four plants in your box, there's just not enough in there to keep you coming back on a regular basis. At least, not for me.

So, it's up to you. There isn't a right or wrong way and the rule keeper inside you may just not be able to defy the plant tag rules. If that's you, as you read this chapter, modify your planting to keep more space between your plants.

Whatever you choose this season, I'd like to dare you, at some point, to join me in planting your garden as full as possible. But you can only do this if you agree to a few things. So, please raise your right hand and take the Intensive Planting Pledge (see page 133) with me.

As you grow from season to season and try various methods, you'll find a rhythm for how much is too much and how little is too little. During some seasons, I wish I'd planted more and, during others, I'm trying to hand off plants to neighbors (I'm currently feeling that way about my kale). But that's part of what keeps it interesting.

Now, let's stop talking about it already and start planting.

There are so many ways to start planting in your kitchen garden: seeds, small plants, tubers, cuttings, bulbs, bare root plants, and more. Before you begin to plant, it's important to know what part of the plant you're hoping to harvest. Is it the root, the shoot, the flower, or the fruit? These parts all correlate with a growing period of the plant. Shoots in the beginning; fruit and seeds at the end.

We'll start by considering what stage of the plant you'll eat. It seems like we're getting ahead of ourselves to be planning the harvest before we even plant. But, beginning with the end in mind is the key to living happily ever after (or at least being happy at the end of the season).

Let's begin with the root. There are many plants we harvest for the root, bulb, or tuber (the part hiding underground), including radishes in the Brassicaceae family and carrots in the Apiaceae family, potatoes in the Solanaceae family, garlic in the Amaryllidaceae family, and sweet potatoes in the Convolvulaceae family. Roots, bulbs, and tubers grow larger as the stem and leaves of the plant grow taller. It's common to think that roots grow first, but plants actually spread down and up simultaneously. Depending on the plant, roots, tubers, and bulbs are often available as early as one month after planting (radishes) and as late as six months or more (garlic).

Just as the root is forming, so is the sprout, this is the newborn form of a plant, fresh from the soil. Sprouts are super nutritious and, usually, the first delicious taste of spring.

Plant Part	Time Required	Sample Plants
Root, Tuber, Bulb	30 to 180 days	Beet, Carrot, Garlic, Onion, Potato, Radish
Sprout	30 to 45 Days	Kale, Lettuce, Mustard, Spinach, Swiss Chard
Stem and Leaves	30 to 75 Days	Herbs, Kale, Lettuce, Mustard, Spinach, Swiss Chard
Bud and Flower	60 to 90 Days	Beans, Broccoli, Cauliflower, Cucumber, Hibiscus, Okra, Peas, Squash
Fruit	60 to 100 Days	Beans, Cucumber, Eggplant, Pea, Pepper, Squash, Tomato, Zucchini
Seed	100+ Days	Corn, Grains, Millet, Sunflower

Sprouts usually occur within days of planting and can be enjoyed within weeks (we're talking fourteen to twenty-eight days after sowing). Our favorite plants to eat in this form are greens in the Asteraceae and Brassicaceae families. We also love asparagus (previously in the Amaryllidaceae family and we will leave it there for convenience's sake).

After the sprout follows the main stem and the first few true leaves. Again, the plants we like to eat in this form are in the aster, brassica, and the Lamiaceae families. We also enjoy the greens in the Apiaceae and the Amaranthaceae families. Leaves are often ready to harvest after the first month of growth and can often be cut from the plant again and again. Prolific is the way to describe the harvests. (This is why I told you start with greens in the last chapter).

Generally speaking, most foods that you'll grow for the root or tuber, the sprout, or the initial stem or leaves will be planted by seed or tuber or bulb and started directly in the ground where the plant will grow to maturity. Most of these plants would be too disturbed by moving them at these young stages to transplant into your garden.

After the plant has grown strong with a main stem and lots of leaves, it will likely begin the process of flowering. Think of flowers a little like puberty for people (without all the drama). Flowers are a sign that the plant is preparing to reproduce. Not all flowers produce fruit to hold their seeds, but many will. Believe it or not, some plants won't get to flower before we eat them as the flower bud is what we eat. These include the Brassicaceae plants broccoli and cauliflower.

Once the flowers open, we may actually want to eat them, too—okra and hibiscus flowers in the Malvaceae family, squash and cucumber flowers in the Cucurbitaceae family, and pea and bean flowers in the Fabaceae family are all edible.

After the flower, many plants produce fruit. The plants in the Solanaceae, the Cucurbitaceae and the Fabaceae families all produce fruit that will encase their seeds for reproduction. In these plant families, we eat the classics: beans, cucumbers, eggplant, peas, peppers, squash, tomatillo, tomatoes, and zucchini. Is your mouth watering? These are the fruits of summer and they all take at least two months before you can harvest them, and some require three or more months to finish production. Good things take time, right?

And, finally, after the fruit is the seed. The seed is the DNA center for this amazing plant that has just finished its life cycle in a very short period of time, going from very small seed to large plant with stems and leaves and flowers and fruit and now creating dozens, if not hundreds, if not thousands, more of itself through seeds. The plants we eat the seeds of are chia, corn, millet, sunflowers, and wheat and grains. To get to seed, most of these plants need more than 100 days to finish growing—and a permanent spot in your garden for the season.

For plants grown for their flower, fruit, or seed, it's generally acceptable, and even best practice, to start seeds indoors or buy small plants from a local nursery or farmer. Because you harvest from the plant at a later stage in its life, it gives the plant a head start, either indoors or under a professional's care before moving into your garden. The further down the lifecycle the harvest, the more time necessary for growth.

This whole "understanding the phase of the plant you want to eat" stuff may have felt like a distraction, but knowing which part of the plant you'll harvest will help you make plans to know how to plant it.

Planting Plan

It's time to take the planting plan you've developed and decide what source you'll use to acquire and start each of those plants you'll be planting. Will you start indoors, directly in the garden, and will you start by seed or by transplant?

If all else fails, or if you've simply spent all your kitchen garden budget on the setup (no shame), start with seeds. Seeds are the least expensive but, sometimes, the most challenging way to start plants. It's like starting a piece of art with a blank sheet of paper, or better yet, with pulp from a tree, versus buying a color by number.

With the seed, it's mostly up to you—the planting, the watering, the light, all of it. If you've ever had a puppy or a kitten or a human baby, you know that the most fragile time of life is the very beginning (read: the stress I felt for the first five years of motherhood).

DETERMINE SEEDS *or* PLANTS

Season	Seeds	Cuttings	Tubers	Bareroot	Plants
Cool	Carrots, Lettuce, Peas	Herbs	Asparagus, Rhubarb	Strawberries, Artichokes	Broccoli, Cauliflower
Warm	Arugula, Basil, Beans, Cucumbers, Squash, Zucchini	Herbs	Potatoes	Berries	Eggplant, Peppers, Tomatoes
Hot	Basil, Beans, Cucumbers, Corn	Herbs	Sweet Potatoes	None	Eggplant, Okra, Tomatillos

But still, as with puppies and baby humans, watching something grow from a tiny speck into an overflowing and fruiting vine in a relatively small amount of time may be the best show you've ever had a front row seat for.

Seed growing is challenging, but it is pure magic.

Seeds

You've taken so much care to set up your kitchen garden. So, don't just run to the hardware store and grab a few seed packets from the nearest kiosk. Trust me, I've done this, and the story did not end well.

Seeds may seem like the most insignificant aspect of this whole kitchen garden thing, but they probably run a close second to soil as most important. Ironically enough, seeds will be your least expensive purchase, even if you take care to order the highest quality available.

A while back, I met with a new soil company that asked me for advice on growing their brand. I quickly encouraged them to collaborate with a great seed company.

"You can have the best soil in the world but if the seeds aren't good it won't matter."

I'm not sure they took my advice but I, of course, thought it was brilliant. I was speaking from experience.

Seeds contain all the things. If you've been impressed with the increasing amount of technology we can now fit into smaller and smaller devices, you're not going to believe what a minuscule seed contains. It's got all the plant's data inside: what season it should sprout; how tall and wide it should grow; the shape of its leaves; its way to find food and nutrients; how to fend off predators and protect itself from disease; and the plan to reproduce itself, by itself, a million times again.

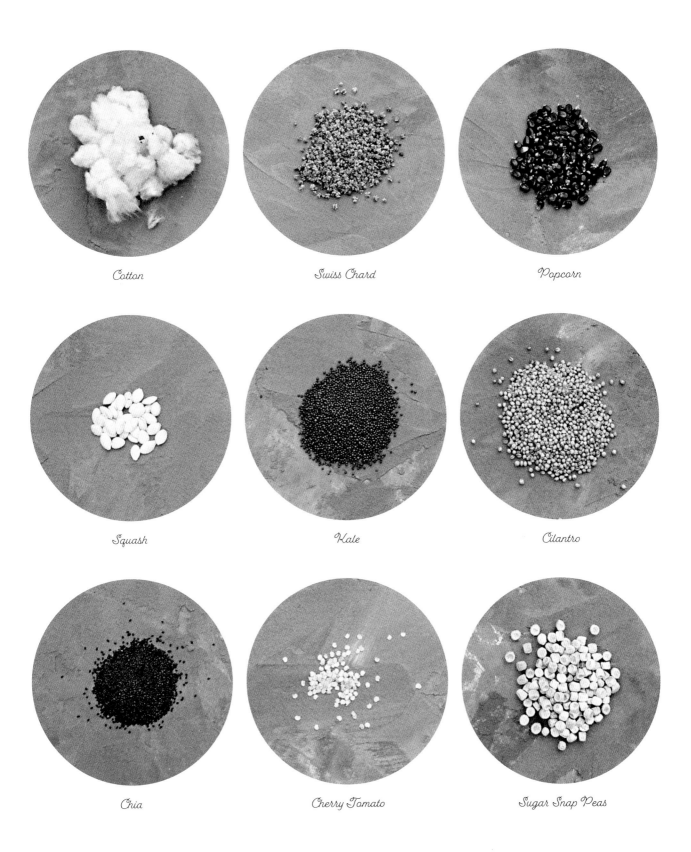

Cotton

Swiss Chard

Popcorn

Squash

Kale

Cilantro

Chia

Cherry Tomato

Sugar Snap Peas

In seeds versus microchips, the seeds would win every day. (Last time I checked, microchips can't have babies.)

But here's the thing: Not just any seed will do.

Even after creating the proper setup, there'd be the—occasional—moment of weakness when I'd grab a few seed packages on my way out of the hardware store, rip open the packages, and follow the instructions for planting spacing and depth (more on that in a minute) and then water it all in.

Though I had the soil and water right, there wasn't one sign of any sprouted seed.

Fast forward a few years and, on the advice of a friend, we ordered seeds from a heritage seed company they loved. The company promised naturally and organically grown seeds and a wide variety of plants I'd never seen before. The seed catalog was crazy big, but we finally made our selections and placed our order.

A few days later, the seeds arrived and, before I could take care to make sure they were properly spaced and dug and perfect, my kids opened several of the packages and sprinkled them like confetti in our raised beds. All hope was lost.

But—in just a few days—every single one of those seeds was up and growing. Over the years and the seasons, I've seen the difference between seeds' performance in my own and all our clients' gardens, and I can almost always trace it back to the source.

Unless you're in need of extra disappointment in your life, remember this as you buy and select your seeds. Seeds should be as locally sourced as possible, naturally or organically produced, and planted as close to their packaging date as possible.

It's best to pay attention to the zones and growing regions and times for the seeds you're after. When you purchase seeds produced in your growing area, the chances of your seeds settling right in and feeling at home in your kitchen garden are much higher. Being someone who's moved quite a bit, I know what it can feel like to try to put down roots in a new place with new weather and new surroundings. It's not easy. Seeds are stressed by change, too. If their parents or grandparents lived in a warm and temperate place, they may suffer when they land in your cooler conditions.

Finding "certified organic" seeds may prove difficult. The goal is finding seeds that weren't raised on plants heavily sprayed with insecticides or fertilizers. All that exposure to synthetic chemicals as they're developing can affect a seed (not to mention the environment) in many ways. Think about nature, and find seeds grown in a situation as close to natural as possible.

Some seeds remain viable a few years after packaging, but you'll find a much higher success rate if you plant fresher seeds. Sorry to say it again, but, think about nature. Seeds that drop from their mother plant settle into the soil and wait a prescribed time period before the right conditions arrive to stimulate germination. As soon as everything is just right, the seeds wake up and sprout.

Most times, not even a year has passed between their falling to the soil and their waking up to a new life. This is the code that's written in their DNA. Imagine how sitting in an envelope on your shelf, season after season after season, affects the viability of a seed. It just wasn't meant to be. So prioritize your newest seeds as you plant.

Now that you've got great seeds, it's time to wake them up and get them growing.

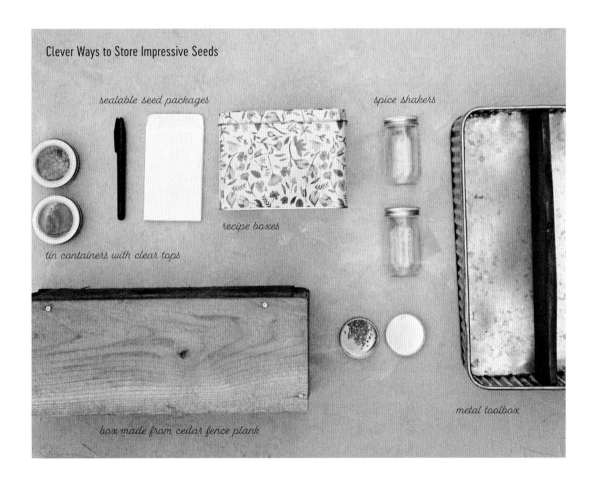

Clever Ways to Store Impressive Seeds

sealable seed packages

spice shakers

recipe boxes

tin containers with clear tops

box made from cedar fence plank

metal toolbox

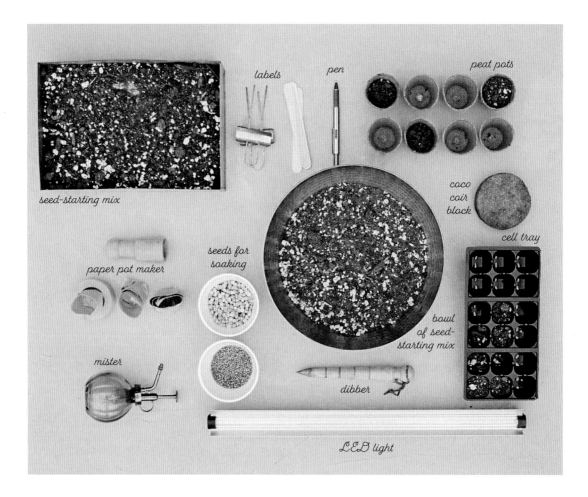

seed-starting mix · *labels* · *pen* · *peat pots* · *coco coir block* · *cell tray* · *paper pot maker* · *seeds for soaking* · *bowl of seed-starting mix* · *mister* · *dibber* · *LED light*

Planting Seeds

There are essentially two ways to plant seeds: indoors and directly into the garden. When you start seeds indoors in containers, you're providing a nursery for your seeds, a protected environment where you can monitor or change the light, the temperature, the exact soil mixture, and more. But, in many cases, direct seeding is easier, more efficient, and more economical. Let's discuss the pros and cons of both methods.

Indoors

To start seeds indoors, you need to purchase some equipment.

Containers

There are all sorts of seed-starting containers on the market and some will make your life a little easier. The classic nursery tray, with cell packs and a clear dome, is something I avoided buying for a long time because it just seemed like so much plastic. But, over time, I realized it really did simplify the seed-starting process and I could re-use those materials.

Lights

If you're anything like me, you're going to hope and pray you can just place your seeds near a windowsill and not worry about setting up lights for your seedlings. Also like me, you'll soon realize that method doesn't work well. Again, think about nature. Most seeds respond to increasing amounts of light and heat to germinate and seedlings need both of these to thrive and grow. Unfortunately, it's quite hard to get enough light through a window for most of the plants we grow and eat. This is where grow lights can help. Even if it's just one tabletop light, purchase one to encourage your seedlings to grow.

Water

Setting up a watering system for your seed starting is essential to success. The best method enables you to water from below—not above—so as not to disturb the seeds. My preference is to have a tray under the seed-starting container that is regularly filled with water. The tiny plants draw up the water from their roots and continue to get all the moisture they need to keep growing.

Soil Medium

The medium you need to start seeds indoors is a little different than the 103 mixture you'll use in your beds. In fact, this is the only time I do purchase pre-made seed-starting soil mix from the nursery. Before filling your containers with the soil mix, soak it and get it nice and wet before proceeding. The goals for your seed-starting medium are that it's light and fluffy, it's sterilized (meaning no weed seeds will grow from it and it contains to harmful pathogens), and that it has relatively low nutrients that can burn young seedlings.

Heat

Seeds are like people: they're temperature sensitive. When it's cold, they crawl under the blankets and hide. Not only that, seeds from different families sprout at different temperatures. The Solanaceae family, for example, sprouts when the soil is much warmer than the much lower temperatures needed for plants from the Brassicaceae family. This is why you might need heat to get your seeds started. You can improvise (I've been known to place my plants on the dryer on the off chance I'm doing laundry), but the pros know you need a heat mat to place your seed trays on. Electric heat mats warm the soil to about 10°F (about 6°C) above room temperature—perfect for initiating seed germination.

Add water to the potting soil mix and mix in thoroughly.

Fill the cells to the top with moistened soil mix.

Using a dibber, make the planting hole to the proper depth.

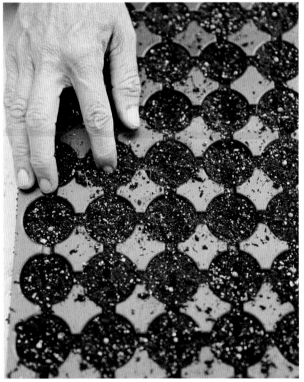

Place the seeds at the proper depth in each hole.

START PLANTS *from* SEED

1. Make or purchase seed-starting mix and moisten it.

2. Fill seed containers with seed-starting mix.

3. Use a dibber to make each planting hole.

4. Place a seed into each cell.

5. Lightly cover the seeds with the seed-starting mix.

6. Cover the seed tray with the clear plastic dome.

7. If watering from the bottom, fill the lower tray with water and let it wick up through the soil.

8. After the seeds sprout, remove the clear plastic top and place the seedlings under a grow light.

You'll need to tend your indoor plants often, ensuring they get adequate light and stay hydrated. If plant stems start to stretch tall and get a "leggy" look, it's time increase the light or get it closer to your plants. Once the plants reach a height equal to the size of the cell and develop several leaf sets, it's time to move the plants into larger pots. If the weather is not yet ideal to move them outdoors, carefully transplant your plants into bigger pots and keep them inside under lights.

As soon as the temperatures begin to match what's necessary for your particular plant, moving your plants outdoors—but not too quickly.

There's a process for getting your indoor plants outside in a gradual manner, called "hardening off." I had no clue about this when I first started gardening and proudly brought my new seedlings I'd babied for a month out into the garden and planted them right away. I'm sad to report that, in less than 24 hours, the little plants shriveled and died.

The indoors is a tame place and the outdoors . . . it just isn't. It's your job to introduce your plants to outside temps, wind, and direct sunshine slowly. You'll do this by moving your plants outdoors for a small amount of time and then returning them indoors, gradually increasing the amount of time they spend outdoors a little each day. Sound complicated? I think so, too. But it's necessary if you want your plants to live and thrive. After your plants have shown that they can stand up to nature (8 to 12 days later), you can officially move them into the garden full time.

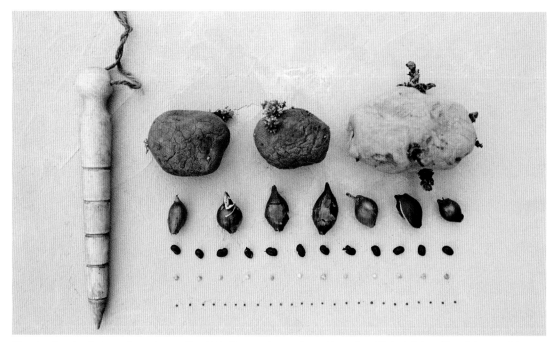

The planting depth depends on the seed's width. Tiny seeds are planted less than ½ inch (about 1 cm) deep and large tubers are planted at least 6 inches (about 15 cm) deep.

If that whole process seems too difficult to you, I have a better plan: Wait to plant your seeds directly into the garden.

Direct Seeding

If the weather is right, you can skip all the complications of indoor seed starting and just place the seeds directly into your kitchen garden soil. This is the way I like to do it and this is the way a lot of plants prefer it.

To direct sow seeds, you need to be like Goldilocks and check for things to be "just right." Seeds are similar to hibernating animals in that they won't wake up until the weather suits them. If you bury them when it's too cold, the wait will seem like forever (and it may very well be) or the seeds may rot before germinating. Conversely, if you bury them when it's too hot, the seeds may rear their heads only to sink back down when they realize the sun is just too bright for their liking.

But, if you get the timing right, direct sowing seeds is the simplest, most straightforward method for getting your plants going. It's the way I first found the most success in the garden: directly sowing lettuce seeds in early fall.

For the most part, plants in the Fabaceae and Cucurbitaceae families don't want to be moved once they've poked their heads out of the soil. They'll perform best if you just plant the seeds right in the ground. I've found that most of the Apiaceae and Asteraceae plants are like this as well. A lot of plants prefer growing this way.

Use a dibber to be certain your seeds are planted to the proper depth—only twice the width of the seed.

Now that you have that trowel in hand, it's oh so tempting to dig a nice deep hole before planting that first seed. I mean, you're a gardener now and gardeners dig, right?

Unfortunately, too much digging is just that: too much. One of the biggest reasons most new gardeners' seeds don't sprout is that they were simply buried too deeply. Seeds are strong, don't misunderstand, but they're not able to claw their way through the Earth's core to make it to the surface.

When a seed is buried too deeply, it just won't make its way to the surface, no matter how much it believes it can. Even if it does, the tiny plant will be so worn out by the time it reaches the sunlight that it begins its life in distress.

All this to say, resist the urge to dig a deep hole. Seeds need only to be planted at a depth that's about twice the seed's width. For example, if a seed is about 1 inch (2.5 cm) in diameter, plant it 2 inches (5.1 cm) deep. If it's ⅛ inch (3 mm), plant it at ¼-inch (6 mm) depth. Ever tried to dig a hole that's ¼ inch (6 mm) deep? It's about as impossible as digging a hole that's 4 feet (1.2 m) deep—but for opposite reasons. For seeds less than 1 inch (2.5 cm) in diameter, simply rake and loosen the soil, place the seeds into a shallow furrow, and lightly sprinkle soil or compost on top. In essence, you're not digging a hole at all.

Now that we've covered the digging situation, let's do the step by step of direct sowing seeds.

To sow seeds directly:

1. Using a hand rake, level the ground where you're sowing before planting. Seeds can easily wash away or get moved around with the slightest change in elevation (a molehill can definitely feel like a mountain to something that tiny).

2. Water down the soil before planting. It's great to have a moist environment before planting your seeds.

3. Measure the distances. Use stakes and string, or a measuring tape, to plot out how you'll space your seeds and then plant accordingly.

4. Use a dibber to make holes at the right depth, or a hoe to create a furrow. Remember, don't plant too deeply!

5. Place all your seeds before covering any up. Trust me on this one; I've covered up seeds only to forget which holes I'd filled.

6. Lightly cover the holes or furrow with compost or soil. Don't compact the soil and don't pile up the soil. Those seedlings are going to have to work hard to break through the soil's surface. Make it as easy on them as possible.

7. Gently water. Moving forward, don't let the soil dry out. There are exceptions but, for the most part, seeds don't like drying out when they're trying to break out of their shell.

8. Watch the magic. You don't want to miss this. When your seeds break the surface of the soil and start to unfurl, you should feel like a kid in a candy store.

That's it for seeds, quite possibly the most amazing thing you're going to touch in the kitchen garden. Scrolling on your phone may be addictive, but I can promise that if you give seeds a chance, they're going to become something you can't take your hands off. And unlike a scroll through the news or a social channel, watching seeds sprout and grow will always make you feel better about yourself and the world around you.

But, as I mentioned earlier, you may need to start with plants for some, or maybe all, your initial kitchen garden growing. Let's talk next about the ins and outs of growing from transplants.

Plant Selection

When you shop for plants, there are a few things to keep in mind: buy small and young, check the roots and leaves, and ask how the plants were grown.

Many of the same principles that held for buying seeds also apply to buying plants. Purchase plants grown as locally and naturally as possible and you'll have more luck if you buy them when they're younger.

Buying locally grown plants is just as important, if not more so, for plants than for seeds. Plants grown locally are so much more likely to thrive in your garden, not to mention your purchase supports small and local businesses. You can find more local plants by shopping at local nurseries than big box stores. You should always ask the nursery or plant center where and how their plants were grown. Even if the answer is that the plants were grown far away from your home, the question is still important. The more we all ask questions that show we care about locally grown seeds and plants, the more retailers will take note.

If finding locally grown plants doesn't seem like challenge enough, now also ask if the plant you're eyeing was grown naturally.

Here are a few ways to ask this question:

1. Was this plant grown naturally? (the obvious option)

2. Did you use any synthetic fertilizers or pesticides on these plants?

3. Do you know about the growing process for this particular plant?

4. Do you have any plants that were grown organically?

Heads up: Retailers can get a little defensive at this point, at least that's been my experience. But, again, the questions matter. If more of us ask, then more stores and growers will act based on our preferences.

Beyond finding naturally grown plants, it's important to purchase plants at the best stage of their growth. It's tempting to buy very mature, large plants already flowering or producing fruit, but you'll generally have better luck if you buy a plant that's more moderately sized, something more like a tweenager instead of a grown adult. A key clue to your plant's age is the roots: Lift the plant out of the pot and check the roots. If they are wrapped tightly around the inside of the pot and/or turning brown, this is generally a sign the plant is too mature for purchase. After checking the roots, check for fruit. If the plant is already producing loads of flowers and fruit from a small plant in a tiny pot, it's likely not going to make the transition to your garden very well. Though it's not as impressive now, opting for a smaller, younger plant increases your chances of success later.

Once you've picked your plants, get them home, watered, and under shade as quickly as possible. "Baby" these plant babies until you can get them planted, which should be as

soon as possible (assuming the weather is right). Nurseries care for plants in small pots daily, but we can easily forget to do so when we get them home. Make it your goal to transfer your plants pronto.

Though you'll generally secure the majority of your garden from either seed or plant, there are a few other options for planting out your kitchen garden.

Tubers and Roots

If planting potatoes, these are generally begun with "seed potatoes" rather than plants. Seed potatoes are simply small potato tubers planted into the ground. The planting process is fairly simple and straightforward: just take a potato, cut it into several sections (each containing an "eye"), and then dig a deep hole and plant the seed potato with the eye pointed up.

Sweet potatoes are planted from slips, or sprouts, grown directly from the tuber. The tuber will naturally develop sprouts, but you can force the process by placing the bottom half of the tuber into a glass of water. It will grow roots down into the water and form several sprouts from the top, which can be cut off the tuber (be sure to keep a piece of the tuber attached to the base of the sprout) and planted directly into the garden when the weather is optimal (remember, sweet potatoes are a hot season plant).

Cuttings

To start new plants from cuttings, severed stem pieces are rooted in water, or in potting soil. Once these cuttings grow roots, they're essentially bareroot plants that can be moved out to the garden as soon as the garden is ready for them. Woody herbs in the Lamiaceae family are perfect for this, as well as rooted cuttings from tomato offshoots.

Bareroot Plants

Generally speaking, there are few bareroot plants you'll add to the kitchen garden, but you may plant crops such as rhubarb or asparagus as bareroots. Bareroot plants are just that: naked plants, with no soil on the roots. Bareroot plants are ordered and shipped from nurseries, and only certain plants can handle the stress of being stored, shipped, and planted bareroot. Planting bareroot plants typically occurs in early spring, but fall is sometimes another option. Fruit trees and berry bushes are also commonly purchased as bareroot plants.

Installing Plants

For each plant, dig a hole that's the same depth as your plant and about twice as wide as the root mass. Don't bury your plant too deeply but, instead, "plant up to the neck of the plant."

The neck is generally the spot where the root becomes the stem. You'll often know it's the neck because that's the general spot where the potting soil begins, but sometimes this isn't the case and you'll need to adjust the soil level either a little higher or a little lower.

The one exception to planting at the "neck" is when planting tomatoes. For those, dig a much deeper hole and bury several inches of stem below the ground, pinching off any leaves that would otherwise get buried. The unique structure of the tomato allows its stem to form new roots and build a stronger plant. But don't try this trick with other edibles or you'll return to find your beautiful plants suffocating.

METHODS (OTHER THAN PLANTS) *for* PLANTING

seeds started indoors

sweet potato tuber

onion bulbs

fresh seeds for direct sowing

rooted cuttings

seed tape for direct sowing

Did I mention that I haven't lived in the same house for more than five or so years since I turned eighteen? It hasn't been easy.

The good thing about all of this moving is that it's given me loads of empathy for my plants when I carry them from one spot to another. I know what it feels like to start over in a completely new place, look down at my feet, and wonder what the heck I'm doing here (again).

Moving is hard, and when you move your plants from one spot to the other, you've got to empathize with what they're going through. Don't move plants when they're too young or too mature. Just as traveling or moving with a newborn or a great-grandmother is more difficult, plants will be more challenged if they're replanted or moved at extreme stages of their growth.

Planting Your Kitchen Garden

You've now got everything gathered: seeds, seedlings you grew yourself (wow!), plants from the store, seeds you'll directly sow, and, maybe, something fancy like a tuber. It's finally time to get all these into the garden.

Before you place your plants and seeds, be sure to pull out the hose or turn on your watering system. Water your soil, water your plants, water yourself. You're all going to need to stay hydrated throughout this process. Your plants will do better if watered well before moving and your garden will take better care of your new plants if it's been recently cared for, too. Ensure the soil is moist and healthy before planting.

First, begin in the centermost part of the garden if the garden is accessible from all sides. If it's a border garden (see page 30), begin in the back. Plant the largest plants first, particularly the ones that need to be near your trellises or supports. Then, head to the next row with the medium-size plants. These can be planted in front of the large plants in a border garden and on either side of the center trellises if you have a square or rectangular garden.

Next, it's time to plant your smallest plants in the front row of your garden. After planting your smallest plants, it's time to plant the border of the garden (if there's room).

My favorite thing to do is plant the border of the garden with perennial herbs and annual flowers. Planting herbs and flowers along the borders not only adds consistent beauty as

PLANTING ORDER

1. Plant large plants.

2. Plant medium plants.

3. Plant small plants.

4. Plant seeds.

5. Plant the borders with perennial herbs and annual flowers.

your bush and vining plants grow larger, they also serve the important role of welcoming pollinators to your kitchen garden. You'll need bees, butterflies, and more friends to help all these plants you're planting flourish, and herbs and annual (and sometimes edible) flowers are just the thing to welcome your new best buddies to the kitchen garden.

After you've planted all this, it's time to add the seeds. The trick with planting seeds and plants together is that you'll have to watch your plants and ensure their leaves aren't blocking the sun for your newly planted seeds (remember the Intensive Planting Pledge [see page 133]?). As long as you've provided the space necessary and the conditions are right, your seeds should begin to show themselves very soon.

Small plants include lettuces and radishes

Medium plants include peppers, beans, and carrots

Large plants include broccoli, tomatoes, and eggplant

Extra-large plants include rhubarb, melons, corn, and sweet potato

PLANTING TIPS

» Water both the plant and the garden first.

» Dig a hole equal in depth to the plant and twice as wide.

» Bury the plant up to its neck (unless it's a tomato, then bury it deeply).

» Gently fill in the hole with garden soil and pat around the base of the plant.

» Lightly water in the plant.

» Cross your fingers that it works!

Summary

Planting a garden is a little like burying a treasure; even after planting hundreds of gardens, I still wonder how this season's plants will do. And every season there are surprises and disappointments. I'll work desperately hard for one harvest and get nothing and then do very little for another plant and be overwhelmed with the outcome. The truth about gardening is that we never know how it's going to turn out.

I think that's why I, and now you, just can't get enough of the experience. The mix of careful planning, hard work, and the need for a little bit of luck, good fortune, or God's smile creates an addictive experience, perhaps the best and most wholesome thrill you can get in your own backyard.

Remember how I said your food would become a wonder? Well, keep your eyes open because these seeds and plants are about to amaze you. But the thrill only happens when you close this book, make a plan, and start planting.

So, gather your impressive seeds and head to the plant store. Yes, you may finally go shopping. As soon as you dig in, you're going to wonder exactly what to do next. And that is exactly what you'll learn in the next chapter.

Opposite: This is a Rooted Garden client's newly planted border kitchen garden with large plants along the trellis (tomatoes), medium plants in the center (peppers and beans), and small herbs and annual flowers in the front (marigolds, angelonia, basil, thyme, and more).

CHAPTER SEVEN
TEND
How to Care for Your Kitchen Garden

● ● ● ● ● ●

Have you heard that if you talk to your plants, they'll grow better?

I have a better idea: Can the plants just talk to me instead?

Are they growing? Are they dying? Are they finishing or just beginning? We could know if they'd just talk to us already.

"Hey, I'm about to sprout and am going to need extra attention over the next few days."

"Did you notice I'm holding on to a lot of fruit over here? It's a little heavy and, if you don't pick them soon, my stem's gonna break."

"Hey, friend! Thanks so much for hanging out with me today. You're the best."

"Help! This creep over here is totally bugging me."

"Hello?? I'm so thirsty. Did you notice it hasn't rained in oh, about a week? Can you imagine not drinking for seven days straight? Yeah, it's not a great feeling. How about getting off your phone and giving me water?"

On second thought, as I write it all out, my plants are starting to sound a lot like my kids (excluding the "you're the best" part). Maybe we don't want them talking, after all. In fact, perhaps one reason gardens are such an escape is because the plants don't talk back—at least not audibly. In a loud world, it's a huge relief to have a place to go that's only humming with bees and butterflies, not whining and complaining.

But the truth is, our plants are communicating all the time. They're just doing it in a more subtle way.

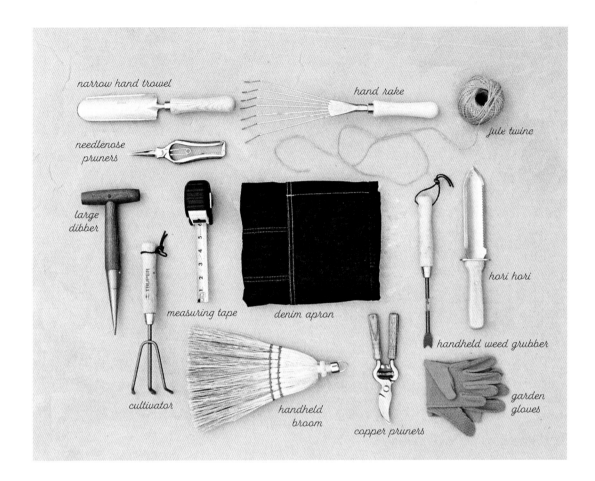

narrow hand trowel

hand rake

jute twine

needlenose pruners

large dibber

measuring tape

denim apron

hori hori

handheld weed grubber

cultivator

handheld broom

copper pruners

garden gloves

Leaves curling, plants standing tall, stems growing 4 inches (10.2 cm) in a few days, fruit turning red, brown spots on leaves, or a flower bowing its head—these are all signs that our plants have something to tell us.

Quiet as they may be, what plants have made clear is that they've got growing phases and challenges just like us. They start small, grow fast, and work hard to reproduce before their season ends. Here's the good news: They want to live, to thrive, and become the biggest and most productive versions of themselves.

As you tend your plants, remember they have the will to live so—no matter what happens—don't feel like it's you versus plants. Your job is to listen to them, work alongside them, and clear the way for your plants to do their thing.

Tending the garden, the middle part of this journey, may feel overwhelming. The newness has worn off and challenges set in (and you're not yet holding a harvest basket).

Tending Notes

As a soccer mom with four kids, I've watched a few games. I still don't know much about the sport, but I do know we're in trouble when our team keeps hanging out on the other team's end of the field. Even though most of my kids are great at playing defender and the goalie is catching everything that comes her way, I can feel my nerves tingle when we can't seem to move the ball toward the opponent's goal for any length of time. No matter how hard we fight, if we're always on the defense, we're probably going to lose the game. I know, I know—playing sports is about building character, notwinning—but soccer moms know best: winning is more fun.

I'll tell you what I'd tell my kids (if they would listen): Stay on the offense as much as you possibly can. It doesn't just apply to soccer but to gardening, too. Your job in tending is to keep the activity on the positive side, the offensive side, the growing side. Because, when you start hanging out on the other side: plant diseases, the dried up soil, the pests, when it's just one defensive move after another, it's inevitable there's going to be a point scored—and it won't be yours.

So, each time you approach your garden, think offense. Think about scoring, about moving the ball—I mean the plants—a little closer to the goal. The more you think about that, the less you will worry about fighting off the bad guys. Hint: You're going to win!

There are a number of ways to play offense in your garden and they can be summed up in this way: feed, support, and prune. The one act of defense you'll have to play is to protect. You'll quickly see all these tasks are, in fact, connected.

NATURAL SOURCES *of* PLANT NUTRIENTS

» Plants/Cottonseed/Nitrogen

» Animal/Castings and Manure/Nitrogen

» Animal/Blood Meal/Nitrogen

» Rock Dust/Phosphorus

» Animal/Bone Meal/Phosphorus

» Animal Manure/Phosphorus

» Sea/Fish Emulsion/Nitrogen

» Sea/Sea Kelp/Potassium

Feed

You adopt a puppy. Or the kitten comes home. What's the first thing you do besides make them a bed? Get food, right? And lots of it. We know animals need to eat regularly and, the younger the animal, the more frequently (ask any mom of a toddler). Many times, we can be so busy thinking about our plants feeding us we forget that our plants need to eat, too. Good news: If you've up set things as you've learned here, your plants are already getting lots of nutrients from the 103, basking in the sunshine, and drinking plenty of water. But just as no animal has only one meal, your plants would really appreciate it if you feed them more regularly, too.

Fig. 1. Add granular fertilizer as a side dressing by gently disturbing the soil around the established plant.

Fig. 2. Follow instructions to place the right amount of nutrients around the base of the plant (don't overdo it).

Fig. 3. Cover the fertilizer with a little soil and water in deeply.

Speaking of toddlers, humans start their life on milk and simple foods and slowly graduate to much more exciting things, like pizza and tacos. Plants also need different nutrients and foods as they grow up (too bad plants can't eat tacos).

Whatever the plant's life stage, we have to (you knew this was coming) think about nature. Don't assume all this talk about feeding plants is a suggestion to purchase something synthetic to add to the garden. Instead, do your best to imitate nature and use materials harvested from nature in a responsible way.

Forms of Plant Food

There are a few forms of naturally occurring food that carry plants from the beginning to their productive end. These include plant-based fertilizers, such as compost and ground seed meals, animal-based fertilizers such as worm castings, manures, and blood and bone meal, mineral resources such as rock dust and green sand, and sea nutrients such as kelp meal and fish emulsion.

One key reason not to use an all-purpose fertilizer with high counts for all the major nutrients is because plants have different nutrition needs at each phase of growth. Commercial products are marketed to our busy lives, proposing a solution that's cheap, fast, and easy. The "one and done method" sounds great on a commercial but the plants aren't buying it.

When your seeds or plants first settle in, the main goal is a healthy and green start. We're aiming for lots of roots and a strong main stem. It's the foundation of the plant we're concerned about at this point, and the best way to encourage strong roots and stems is first to give your plant healthy, wonderful soil (you've done that already!).

Mycorrhizae is a naturally occurring fungus that connects roots to the nutrients in soil. This connection happens on its own, but adding a little mycorrhizae to the soil around your plants as they begin to grow may help establish the connection a bit faster.

The other nutrients necessary to build these plant parts are mostly nitrogen and potassium. Nitrogen comes from a variety of sources, most being that 4 percent mentioned in the soil chapter, including earthworm castings, but also organic cottonseed meal, and kelp meal. For each of these, follow the directions when applying them, being certain not to apply too much. Chicken manure can be used as well but you'll have to be especially careful not to burn the young plant at this stage of their growth. Potassium comes right behind nitrogen in order of importance. Potassium determines the root health of your plants, their ability to grow big, and to take up water and nutrients. Green sand and kelp meal are both great sources of potassium for plants.

Once a strong root structure and sturdy main stem are growing, it's time to focus on leaf growth. For some plants, like lettuce and kale, this may be your end goal. Because the plant is stronger and more established at this point, you can use stronger nitrogen sources, like chicken and rabbit manure.

For fruiting plants, once the plant starts to produce a good number of leaves and has a strong stem, it's time to encourage flowering and fruiting. This is accomplished with phosphorus. Though we like to call them "vegetables," most of the foods we think of eating from the garden are technically "fruits." And fruit follows flowers. Before flowers can become fruit, most will need to be pollinated. Bees, butterflies, and other insects often do this work for us. (An important reason to include pollinator-friendly plants in your planting plan.) But you can assist the insects by hand pollinating. Use a clean paintbrush, gather pollen from male flowers (those with a straight stem) and then tap into female flowers (those with a more curved stem).

Once the flowers turn to fruit, continue to feed your plant phosphorus-rich foods, such as rock dust, bone meal, finished animal manures.

Support

Now that your plants are fed, it's time to support them as they grow. Once your plants have sprouted or taken up their spot in your kitchen garden, be sure they know they've got someone to lean on.

First take care that each plant has enough soil around their roots. A plant's roots should never be exposed, but certain plants benefit from having additional soil around their roots. These include potatoes, tomatoes, beans, and some root crops. Farmers call it "hilling." In fact, farmers will go along a row, take a hoe, and push the soil up on the plant all along the row, essentially forming a long hill. This gives the plants extra support as they grow and encourages the plants to produce better. For beets, carrots, and other root crops, hilling keeps the "shoulders" of the roots from turning green.

Beyond support at the base, some plants need support above ground as well. Some plants that don't quite need a trellis in the garden but still require a vertical support of some kind. Included in this category are peppers, eggplants, tomatillos, and possibly even broccoli, cauliflower, or kale. These large and lengthy plants don't necessarily vine but still get quite tall.

Without a support, plants may fall over and break in a storm or just collapse due to the amount of weight they're carrying, and a collapsed branch is a very sad thing. When you use a stake, you'll also need twine or a gentle support that won't harm your plant to attach it. Place stakes right next to your plants and bring twine and scissors with you as you tend the garden to tie the stem to the stake regularly as it grows.

Beyond stakes, trellises are necessary for any vining plants, such as tomatoes, cucumbers, peas, pole beans, and winter squash. Although beans and cucumbers develop tendrils to attach to the trellis, winter squash may need to be tied to it. Each time you tend your garden, connect the newest growth on your vining plants to the next level of trellis with twine.

Prune

Warning: If you're uncomfortable with being bossy this may be a stretch for you but, if you really wish you could shout orders, and someone, anyone, would listen, you're going to love this part of tending the garden.

For simplicity sake, I'm taking liberty with the word "prune" to mean any way you clear out part of your plants. This includes thinning your plants at the beginning of their life cycle to clipping the top of the plant when you know the season is about to end, and everything in between.

If you follow my intensive planting plan, you remember that a garden planted this closely must be regularly pruned and thinned, but even if you're the rule-following type and you spread out your plants as the plant tags require, you'll still see benefits from pruning.

Thinning Plants

Many times, after starting a plant from seed, it's important to return to the seedlings when they're young and thin out the plants. If plants are grown from seed that was planted too densely, they won't have enough room to develop to their full potential.

The most common plants that will need thinning at the seedling stage include plants in the Apiaceae, Asteraceae, Brassicaceae, Cucurbitaceae, and Fabaceae families.

The way to thin a plant is to imagine it fully grown, in the shape you buy from the grocery. For instance, think of a carrot. If you'd like your carrot to be about 2 inches (5.1 cm) wide at the top, you need to be sure each carrot sprout is at least 2 inches (5.1) from the next carrot sprout. If you want to harvest lettuce heads 8 inches (20.3 cm) in diameter, you need that lettuce you planted, you guessed it, at least 8 inches (20.3 cm) from the next plant.

Once you know the spacing required, you next have to do the difficult task of selecting which plants to remove and which to keep. Natural selection is up to you now. To thin an area, you can pluck the entire plant up or cut it off at the soil level. Cutting it at soil level ensures you don't disturb the other roots growing nearby. Plucking it out ensures that no part of the plant will take up any room near your other plants for quite some time (and, if you are like me and can't stand to say goodbye to a plant you worked so hard to grow you can try your luck and replant the thinned plant).

Prune for Growth

The plants that need to be thinned are, interestingly enough, not the ones that need to be pruned. It's mostly the Solanaceae plants, the Lamiaceae plants, and, some of the Cucurbitaceae plants that need a good haircut.

Pruning has at least three purposes. One, it's wonderful for directing the plant's growth and ensuring you get more of what you want and less of what you don't. Two, it's great for dealing with issues and challenges. And three, it feels really good when you've had a stressful day.

I didn't prune my plants in the beginning because I was scared. Cutting something from the plant babies I'd worked so hard to nurture? It just felt wrong. But, then, there was that year I planted twelve tomato plants—and I watered and added natural fertilizer and did all the right things to make them grow. Every single week I'd wrangle the wild branches inside the cage and, oh, so, carefully, tie the vines in hopes that they wouldn't bend or break. The

PLANTS *that Need* THINNING

Arugula, Kale, Radish/Brassicaceae
Beans/Fabaceae
Carrots/Apiaceae
Cucumbers, Squash/Cucurbitaceae
Lettuces/Asteraceae

plants looked so healthy and green. Too green in fact. So green there was no red, no yellow, no orange . . . no tomatoes. I should've harvested pounds of tomatoes but, instead, I just had pounds of leaves.

Enter the following season, when I planted twenty-six tomato plants: two gardens with thirteen plants each (I counted twice) and as soon as the plants were six inches (15.2 cm) tall, I started pruning. Just one little cut to start, but by mid-season, I'd leave the garden with piles and piles of tomato leaves and something else, too: a huge bowl of tomatoes. The difference in production was crazy.

The experiment taught me that my plants and my kids are different on at least one point: My plants like me telling them what to do.

Here's how I prune tomatoes:

1. At the outset of the plant's growth, prune the plant to one main stem by cutting any low leaders that would otherwise form a new vine.

2. Once the plant is about 1 foot (30.5 cm) tall, prune it once a week, starting from the bottom, cutting about one-third of the leaves all the way back to the main stem.

3. Only pinch the suckers from the first few feet of the plant, then allow the suckers to form and grow.

4. Once the plant is as tall as you'd like it to be, or you know the season is ending, prune off the top of the plant so the vine will finish forming and ripening the tomatoes already on it.

RULES *for* PRUNING

1. Use clean pruners. Wipe with rubbing alcohol between pruning each plant.

2. Start with the oldest leaves at the base of the plant and work your way up.

3. Never prune off more than one-third of the total number of leaves.

4. Leave fruiting branches alone; prune branches that produce mostly leaves.

Prune for Defense

Beyond pruning for production, I also prune for protection (I guess it's finally time to play defense).

When dealing with pests or disease, the first tool I recommend using is your pruners, not a spray bottle. Many first-time gardeners have the tendency to spray the minute they see a bug or spots on the leaves. Pruning, however, is the better way to address pests.

The minute I see damage on one of my plants, I grab my pruners. I'll begin with the most damaged leaf and slowly work my way around the plant until I've removed as many of the damaged leaves as possible. If this means I remove every single leaf, it's time to pull up the plant for good. But, if I can manage to cut back just one-third of the plant's foliage and only healthy leaves remain, I'll certainly do it.

1. Have very clean pruners.

2. Start at soil level. Sounds weird to start "pruning" in the dirt, but don't skip this step. Cut or pull away any leaves that have made contact with or dropped to the soil.

3. Move to the bottom of the main stem. The leaves at the bottom of the plant are the oldest and most likely to be attacked by pests or disease, or just simply do not have the same skip in their step they used to. Remove these from the main stem of the plant.

4. Slowly move your way up the main stem of the plant to remove any leaves that are diseased, hold pests, or just don't look awesome, remembering not to remove more than one-third of the plant.

Next, let's discuss what to do for your plants when pests or diseases arrive.

Protect

The old saying goes, "The best fertilizer is the gardener's shadow." But, moreso, it's your presence in the garden that's the best pesticide.

Just like in any game, no matter how hard you play offense, there will come a time when your opponent has the ball and it's time to fight back. Pests, diseases, and difficult weather will all come your garden's way, but that doesn't mean you'll lose the game. Instead, the game just got much more interesting.

If you're wondering which plants you should defend first, take a minute to think about those wild animal documentaries. The leopard or cheetah is coming after the herd. Who gets eaten first? The youngest, the oldest, or the injured. Right? The predators know these are the easiest to catch and the same is true in your garden.

The youngest plants are very susceptible to pest attack or disease. Tender leaves on soft new stalks and tired plants are the favorite target for problems. Plants with injury or disease are already diseased are more likely to house a pest or a problem. If a plant's main stem has broken, it's recently been pruned, or it's been attacked by disease a few weeks ago, it's more than likely going to be attacked again. It's not fair, but it's just the way nature works. (And we're thinking about nature, in case you forgot).

Caterpillars, borers, beetles, aphids, grasshoppers, flies, mealybugs, slugs, whiteflies, oh my! There are literally a million things out there that want to eat your garden as much (or more) than you do. You'll know they've arrived when things go missing off your plants—holes in leaves, stems, or, even, fruit.

Disease can be caused by bacteria, fungi, and viruses. Most diseases are commonly spotted on the plants' leaves and are typically caused by a relationship gone wrong with fungi, which can cause fungal leaf spot and powdery mildew. The second most common diseases are viruses transmitted by, you guessed it, pests.

At the first sign of an attack (discolored leaves, holes in leaves, missing plant parts), the first thing to do is prune (but you knew this already). After pruning, check the soil area and the undersides of the plant's leaves. Oftentimes, pests hide just below the soil's surface or underneath the large leaves in your garden. By checking the soil around your plants and leaves, you may discover the problem and stop it in its tracks. After raking around the plant, add clean compost to the plant's surroundings.

Defense Treatments
Insecticidal Soap

Once you've cleaned the soil area and added compost and identified the pest, it's time to decide if treatment is necessary. If it is, be as gentle with treatment as possible. I like to begin with just an insecticidal soap for most insects, including aphids, beetles, and caterpillars. I spray my plants as little as possible, as I find the sprays rarely work long term, whereas the pruning and regular plant care rarely fail.

Garlic Oil

Insecticidal soap is, typically, the mildest form of pest defense and defends against soft-bodied insects. Garlic oil is the next form of attack I use in our gardens. Sprays and solutions made of garlic oils are a natural way to protect your leaves from critters and even kill adult insects.

Neem Oil

If soap and garlic oil don't do the trick (which rarely happens), I call in the big guns: neem oil. Neem not only minimizes pests but also fights fungus and bacteria. In other words, it's a great way to fight both pests and disease.

Bt Sprays

Bt stands for *Bacillus thuringiensis*. It's a naturally occurring bacteria that disrupts caterpillars' guts to the point they can't eat any more. Appetizing don't you think? This is the strongest spray product I use in the garden and, even at that, I use very little. But, when I need it, I know it works—and very quickly. However, Bt is only effective against caterpillars, like cabbageworms, diamondback moth caterpillars, and tomato hornworms.

Iron Phosphate Baits

To deal with slugs and snails, I use iron phosphate-based products because they're safer to use around kids and pets than synthetic chemical-based slug baits. Diatomaceous earth is another slug control product I sometimes use.

Protective Covers

At times, there will be pests much bigger than caterpillars that these sprays just can't handle. Terrible, horrible pests that shouldn't be named here, but must be for your sake: gophers, moles, rabbits, squirrels, and the like can drive you completely mad in the garden. Spoiler alert: methods you'll find online won't work. The chile powders and the forks in the dirt and the flowers that will, supposedly, repel them? I've tried them all and seem always to attract that one pest that didn't read the internet and know they're supposed to hate marigolds or be scared of CDs or throw up when they eat a tomato covered in hot sauce.

In fact, when it comes to pests—both small and large—the only cure I've found that truly works is a cover for the garden. This can be a formal structure like a protective cage made of hardware cloth and wood or a simpler structure like poles and mesh cloth. Lightweight, translucent row cover fabric is another great option to keep pests off plants. It can be work to create such a cover but, if you're in a place where both big and small pests won't give you a moment's peace, this may be your best solution.

Weather Protection

If pests and disease aren't enough to manage, there's that other thing to be concerned with—weather. (Told you it's more fun to stay on our side of the field).

Too much rain or cold or sun can cause problems in the garden, too. The good news is, if you're planting by families and in line with the proper season suggested in this book, your plants should, generally, be able to endure most of what Mother Nature throws at them.

But, if you want your plants to start earlier or push further into seasons they can't naturally handle, adding weather protection is a great way to make that possible. You can use the same protective covers you've created for pest management for frost, sun, or wind protection, too.

Frost-protective covers do just that: Protect your plants from frost. You can generally get about four extra weeks of planting and growing time on both sides of the cool season by growing under frost covers. Shade covers allow you to stretch cool- and warm-season plants into the hot season by keeping harsh sun off your plants in the heat of the day but still allowing air and water to flow to your plants. You can take it to another level with a greenhouse or poly tunnel but that will have to be for another book.

Summary

There are ways to keep scoring no matter the challenges—be they pests, disease, or harsh weather—you face in the kitchen garden. Remember, it's your shadow in the garden that counts.

Here's how it works. I'll head out to the garden to trellis up a tomato vine. While out there, I'll see damaged leaves, which I'll prune off. And, just as I'm about to leave the plant, I'll see exposed roots, which I'll cover with extra compost and then dig in a little chicken manure right alongside the roots. I'll grab my watering can and water the plant in well and then be on with my day.

Remember chapter 1? The kitchen garden is a space that's tended regularly. Taking care of my kitchen garden plants has become a form of therapy for me, not a chore. There are times you'll need to do major work in the garden, especially if you've been away from it for too long, but, for the most part, the kitchen garden just needs to be touched a little on a regular basis. A weekly prune, a deep water twice a week, some extra compost every weekend, and worm castings once a month. See that pest? Knock it off into soapy water. That plant's not looking so great? I think it's time to remove it.

We should tend the garden the way we tend our bodies and our loved ones—a little each day and all will be okay. If there comes a time when the game feels frustrating and it seems like you're only playing on your opponents' end of the field, focus on the offense. Start kicking a little stronger in the right direction and you'll soon be winning again. Even if you lose a few, at least the game was interesting.

CHAPTER EIGHT

HARVEST

Enjoy Kitchen Garden Growth

● ● ● ● ● ●

It was the first spring after I started Rooted Garden and two of my wonderful new clients offered to throw a party to spread the word. I'm tossing out ideas for the party and trying to sound like I know what I'm doing. I mention a "garden-to-table" event where we could serve just-picked foods and talk about the value of eating locally and seasonally.

The clients, now friends, love the idea.

"Great! Let's call it, a 'Rooted Garden to Table Brunch.'" They invite their friends and nearly thirty sign up. Wonderful!

I call my mom.

Me: "Yep, twenty-six are coming. Isn't that incredible?"

Mom: Silence.

Me: "Mom, won't it be neat to share my business with that many women?"

Mom: Silence.

Me: "Mom, you still there?"

Mom: "Yes, I'm still here but just a little worried for you. You barely cook for your own family. How in the world are you going to cook for thirty women you've never met?"

Me: Silence

There's a reason they say, "Mom is always right." She is.

It's true: I'm a gardener, not a cook. But what mom didn't know was that I wasn't relying on my culinary skills to pull this thing off. I had a secret that would make it successful. But don't think I was too proud to still ask mom for help.

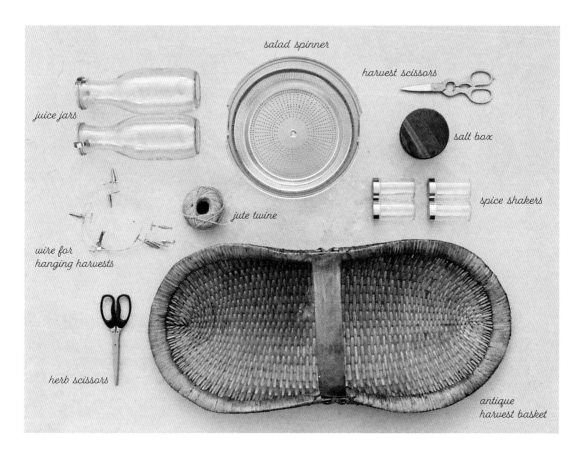

salad spinner

harvest scissors

juice jars

salt box

spice shakers

jute twine

wire for
hanging harvests

herb scissors

antique
harvest basket

Yes, it was true I hadn't thought about the logistics, but I did, in fact, have a plan for the menu. I wasn't aiming to show off my cooking skills, but to show off the food itself, to help these women realize that just-harvested and seasonal food was so very good that even a struggling cook like me could pull together a delicious meal. I was less concerned about the actual dishes and recipes and more concerned that I'd find the freshest, just-harvested ingredients, either from my garden or the gardens of farmers down the street.

Don't worry; I did, eventually, land on a menu. It was early spring so we had sweet potato waffles as an appetizer (sweet potatoes last forever after a fall harvest), roasted beets and carrots, braised arugula with balsamic dressing, and a beet green and kale frittata (I have Barbara Kingsolver to thank for that one), Martha Stewart—inspired rosemary and lavender shortbread with grapefruit halves garnished with mint for dessert (grapefruits grow like crazy in Houston). If all was a flop, I did bring along some juice and Prosecco (the one item not locally sourced).

Even with my plan, of course, I needed my mom. Thankfully, the whole event went off pretty close to perfect, at least as I define it. As the ladies tasted everything, they kept asking for the recipes.

"I love the beets. How'd you cook them?"

"I just used olive oil and sea salt."

"What did you do with this arugula? I've never had it so sweet."

"Olive oil, sea salt, and balsamic vinegar."

"The carrots are divine. How'd you make those?"

"Umm, olive oil and sea salt and balsamic vinegar."

I was sounding ridiculous at this point.

The ladies looked at me confused—how did I cook these things so simply and make them taste so good?

It was clear I'm no chef at Chez Panisse but I did learn this much from Alice Waters: well-sourced, fresh ingredients make the dish.

If it's delicious to start, you don't need much to make it better, just enhance what's already there.

Whether we love or hate cooking, the fact is we all eat. Harvesting and preparing food from the kitchen garden is one of the most satisfying and fulfilling ways to do this thing we call, "meal time."

I'll be the first to admit that I'm not a huge fan of hanging out in the kitchen. But food is one of the kindest things we can give our bodies, our families, friends, and community. It's the absolute kindest when it's food we've grown ourselves, from seed even, right in our own kitchen garden.

Let this chapter be a celebration of all your hard work, a collection of all the careful hours you've dug into that soil of yours, and a huge hand clap for you—the gardener.

Harvest Concerns

"Is it ready?"

"This is much smaller than what I'm used to from the grocery store."

"I'm so scared to pick it. I don't want to mess it up."

Harvesting from your garden can be the same nail-biting experience as planting it in the first place. You've come this far, and it would absolutely stink if you messed it up now. Believe me—I've felt all the feelings.

There was that time when I planted and nurtured a bucket of potatoes and then gathered the kids around to pour out the bounty. With cameras ready, I overturned the bucket only to dump out loads of soil and one lonely potato. French fry, anyone?

Or, the moment I headed out with the basket to pluck all the slicer tomatoes I'd been eyeing, only to find the squirrels had beaten me to it.

There's that time I harvested beans because I knew they were ready but only ended up with six. What to do with six beans? Maybe fix them with that one potato.

Or, that day I was working inside and my daughter was outside playing. A few door slams later, she arrives to the table with dripping and dirty hands.

"I pulled all the carrots, Mommy." (And by all, she means all hundred of them).

"And I washed them all in my bathroom."

Side note: a work deadline, twenty pounds (9 kg) of carrots in your bathroom, and a clogged sink isn't exactly the mind-clearing experience we're going for with a kitchen garden.

For me, the secret to enjoying the garden season after season is celebrating each little thing I get to pick, and not worrying so much about the final outcome. There are the gardeners with big grocery store scales who weigh their harvests and there are those who add up the value of all they've grown. Believe me; I'm impressed. But my focus is more on the small everyday harvests, the things I walk inside with after a moment of tidying the garden.

However you'd like to enjoy your harvests, a little at a time or all at once, the magical part is you're harvesting real, delicious, organic food that you grew yourself.

You! Harvesting! From your garden!

Take a moment to celebrate that wonder and appreciate the fact that such a delightful thing is possible.

Size

The first consideration when you harvest is size.

You want to be certain the plant had enough time to create and finish making that part you're ready to eat. Remember what we learned in chapter 5—roots and shoots and fruits all need a different amount of time to finish the job they've been given: growing.

It might come as a surprise, but you want to harvest when the produce isn't quite as big as those you'd get from the store. Although bigger vegetables are great for the county fair and impressive photos, the general truth is, the smaller the fruit, the better the flavor.

This isn't true for all harvests, but it is true for most. Obviously, there is a limit to this rule, as you want your food to be big enough to be able to cut it up and share. As tasty as a three-inch (7.6 cm) cucumber may be, it isn't really worth the effort for half a bite. But, once a vegetable is large enough in size to eat and enjoy, go ahead and enjoy it. Don't wait until it gets larger or you may miss it entirely.

Okra is one of those things. It grows in the heat of Houston's summer so I would often miss the harvests while I'm away with the kids. I'll never forget the summer I returned home, eager to have a garden meal and harvested all the okra I saw. I found the most delicious okra and tomato recipe and toiled over it for about a half hour (a record length of time in the kitchen for me). I served it proudly and, as my husband and I both took our first bites, we started to chew, and kept chewing. And, then, we chewed more. Five minutes passed and we were still chewing. The flavor was delicious, but the texture was equivalent to— shall we say—cardboard? Okra, once past four or five inches (10.2 or 12.7 cm) in length, becomes extremely fibrous. So much so that, I'd say, it's no longer edible (and I'm sure my husband would, too). We tried to work our way around the cardboard to enjoy the sauce, but the bits of tough okra had spread everywhere and the whole meal was a total waste. Lesson learned. Overripe harvests are only suitable for the compost pile, not your kitchen table.

Consider the typical grocery size of a fruit or vegetable, and then shrink it a bit in your mind. That's the size you're looking for with your harvest.

But here's the challenge: Sometimes there may only be three of those things that are the right size at the same time. Three. What to do with three beans ready to harvest and thirty beans that aren't? Harvest a few, clean them, and store them and have them wait for the rest of their siblings to be ready in a few days. Or, freeze them and add more to the bag as they're ready. Even though you only have a few worth harvesting now, picking the largest vegetables and fruit encourages the plant to finish growing the others. So, go ahead and pick, wash, store, and come back tomorrow to pick more.

Timing

If it's a big harvest, like say, those twenty pounds (9 kg) of carrots or ten pounds (4.5 kg) of tomatoes or a huge load of kale, make sure the timing isn't just right for the garden but also right for you. Pulling up that much food at once depending on how you want to use or store it, it could take a lot of time. In these cases, it's best to wait to harvest until the weekend, or a calmer work night, or a moment when you know you can invite friends or family over to help with the process.

Timing doesn't just matter for the plant and for you but also for the actual time of day. Though plants may not look like they're waking up, stretching, having their coffee, and then moving through their workday

WHEN to HARVEST

Harvest/Size

>> Bell peppers/6 inches (15.2 cm)

>> Carrots/8 inches (20.3 cm)

>> Green beans/5 inches (12.7 cm)

>> Jalapeño peppers/5 inches (12.7 cm)

>> Kale/10 inches (25.4 cm)

>> Lettuce leaves/6 inches (15.2 cm)

>> Peas/4 inches (10.2 cm)

>> Tomatoes, cherry/1 to 2 inches (2.5 to 5.1 cm)

>> Tomatoes, slicer/5 inches (12.7 cm)

the way we do, they do have a daily schedule, too. Just like we sleep when it's dark, our plants renew themselves each night, taking in more moisture, and pulling up nutrients from the soil. Once the sun is up, it's time for the plant to go to work, turning sunlight into food for the next phase of growth.

All this nighttime rest and recovering means, unlike some of your family members, plants are sweetest in the early morning. When harvesting leaves, this is especially true. For most harvests, as soon as you've had your coffee, it's time to head out and start picking. (Take my advice and don't do anything before coffee; it just doesn't go well).

Harvest Methods

When you come to harvest, bring twine, rubber bands, a pitcher of water, and, if you have it, a cooler bag.

Head out to the garden with a basket and pruners. Pick all that looks about one-third smaller than the grocery variety and immediately bring it indoors. Rinse it (preferably not in the bathroom sink), dry it, and then enjoy it or store it in a way that you can enjoy it later. Just as nearly every plant family has its own needs for planting, most have their own way to be harvested, too. For the Asteraceae you're growing for leaves, either cut the leaves from

the outside and bottom of the plant, leaving the plant to regrow from its center, or cut the entire set of leaves from the base with a knife or thick pruners (this would be for a head lettuce), or you can pull up the entire plant from its roots and clean and cut off the roots.

For the Lamiaceae, just harvest the outside and lower leaves or trim the tips of the plants, leaving the heart to continue growing (this is a perennial). For the Solanaceae and Cucurbitaceae, use clean pruners and cut fruits such as tomatoes, peppers, and cucumbers from the stem so as not to harm the plant. The same is true for Fabaceae—the peas and beans. The exception is in the Solanaceae family, where you'll dig the potatoes and pull up the entire plant at once. For Apiaceae and Amaranthaceae, you may either pull the entire plant (in the case of carrots or beets) or just harvest the outer and lower leaves (in the case of dill, parsley, spinach, and Swiss chard).

The goal with the harvest is to catch it early and at its peak while not harming the remaining plant, and to encourage more production. There are few plants you'll completely remove from the garden as you harvest. The majority will be harvested from and left to keep growing.

Enjoy the Harvest

Once you cut your first items from the garden, the tendency may be to let them hang out with you in the garden while you keep playing, but you should send them inside or protect your newly found treasures as quickly as possible.

Grocery stores, in general, stock vegetable and fruit varieties that travel and store well. Most foods from the store need endure for hundreds, if not thousands of miles on a truck, then go through inventory and sit on a shelf for seven to fourteen days before moving to your refrigerator.

The fact is, only some types of fruits and vegetables can survive this kind of handling. It's tough to be plucked from your happy place, carted all over the country, and then forced to sit under fluorescent lights for ten days before being chopped up and eaten. Only a few special breeds can hang on for the challenge, and few of those breeds are growing in your kitchen garden. At least, they shouldn't be. Because, believe me, the better tasting varieties are often the ones that must be eaten immediately after plucking.

The point? Don't pick it and forget it (the way you do with all those veggies currently rotting in your fridge). Eat it or store it as close to immediately as humanly possible. The sooner the better.

There are a number of ways to store your harvests. Refrigerate them, dry them, ferment or can them, eat them, or create a dish with them.

First, rinse your vegetables, (If you've pulled a dirtier harvest such as potatoes, carrots, or radishes, clean them off outside with a hose. For leafy greens, broccoli, or other fruits, submerging your harvest in a deep bowl of ice-cold water is a great way to preserve the fruit and maintain the flavor (plus the ice helps get rid of any pests piggybacking into your harvest basket).

Once you've rinsed your harvest, completely dry it and then wrap and store in the refrigerator, keeping in mind that some fruits will preserve better if kept at room temperature. Some vegetables will last a few days, or even a week or two, this way.

That is nature's way of caring for us. Think about it: Citrus is available in the coldest time of the year, just when we need all that vitamin C to fend off colds. And watermelon is available in the heat of summer, just when we need all that water and hydration. I can't help but think we were meant to burst completely with whatever food is growing wildly at the moment.

Let go of the pressure that everything on your plate needs to be from a garden harvest if one thing is. Even bringing that one item in to add to an otherwise grocery store meal can make a huge difference in taste and help you appreciate the just-harvested freshness from the garden.

One of my first edibles was a pot of chives my mother gave me. I cut from that pot at least once a weekend and added the trimmings to eggs and salads (all bought from the grocery). I was far from "garden to table" but the magic of adding a little bit of freshly harvested chives made the everyday meal feel almost elegant (minus the toddlers screaming in highchairs).

In summer when my spring salads have all finished and I only have the dull grocery store varieties, I'll still add garden basil or mint to spice things up.

Now that we know the basics of harvesting and the when and how, it's finally time to dig in. There are millions of ways to enjoy the food you'll be bringing from your kitchen garden. Here are some ideas to get you going in the very best and most delicious way.

A short list of what you'll need to make the most of your harvests includes salts, different types of vinegar, and oils. I've told clients this short list for years (and it's clearly what I used for the Rooted Garden to Table brunch) but it wasn't until I read, *Salt, Fat, Acid, Heat* that I realized why it works. As Samin notes in her epic book that makes even me think I can cook, these are the key ingredients for any good dish, and they work even better when you just picked that veggie you're smothering with oil, vinegar, and sea salt.

Heat is the element I use the least. (Remember I'm a gardener, not a cook.) Let's first cover the ways to use your vegetables before turning on the fire.

Raw

I think, on the whole, most of us completely underestimate the power of a beautiful spread of raw veggies and fruits on a platter. Perhaps because it seems so simple. But, to me, there is nothing better than a whole plate full of just-harvested vegetables ready for the taking.

I don't know who needs to hear this, but you are absolutely free just to sit right there in the garden and eat until your heart's content. In fact, you should eat as much of your harvests raw as possible. If you've never experienced pulling something off the vine and popping it into your mouth within the span of about 2.4 seconds, I'm not even exaggerating to say, you haven't really lived yet.

Besides, just eating in its rawest form, there's a way to make your raw food taste great without adding much to it and that is by simply cutting and chopping.

I think I learned this from my two years in China, but a good chop can be the difference in just enjoying your harvest and crying because it's so good (especially if you're chopping onions). The vegetables I had in my small town in China were all chopped small and cute and in so many different ways. Every meal there helped me see that chopping made the food taste better—a julienned carrot tastes so much better than a carrot that was just sideways chopped in the traditional fashion. So, grab your knife and start crying over your cute cut veggies too.

Salad

Salad isn't just for lettuce anymore. Salad is simply raw things cut up and put together. There are so many ways to make it good. We all know we should eat more salads but pulling partially spoiled greens from a bag or a plastic box just isn't appetizing. Freshly cut slices of harvests all mixed together is pretty close to perfect, if you ask me.

Try cutting everything the same way so you get a blend of all the flavors.

Sauces, Oils, and Dressing

I am a saucy kind of girl and I don't mean that I speak my mind too much, though that's true, too. But, any blah kind of dish tastes so much better if I can dip it into a saucy kind of sauce, and sauces from the garden can seriously make you feel like a gourmet cook even if all you've ever made is scrambled eggs.

One of the ways I became hooked on the garden to start was making little sauces from fresh parsley or cilantro or dill. Chimichurri made from parsley is pretty close to divine. Tzatziki made from dill and salsa with cilantro are just perfect. Even if everything else on your plate is blah, the sauce will make the dish.

Spices

Another simple way to enjoy your harvest is to create homegrown spices. Red pepper flakes, coriander, garlic and onion powder, dried stevia, all can come from your kitchen garden, and the taste will be so much better than even the organic varieties you buy from the store.

Infusions

Herb-infused oils are the simplest way to use your herb harvests—all you have to do is, literally, place some herbs in some oil. By immersing clean herbs or vegetables into oil, the flavors slowly come together. Generally, you'll heat the oil and then pour the liquid over your clean and dried garden harvests. Let the flavors meld together for a few days and then strain the harvested item from the oil.

Infused vinegars are delicious, too. You can infuse vinegar with chive blossoms and hot peppers.

Salt and Sugar Blends

You can also make unique salt and sugar blends. I've mixed oregano and rosemary and all sorts of fragrant herbs with salt, and the new herb flavor can make any dish feel more fresh and gardenlike. It makes me feel very much like a professional chef.

Garnish

In the West, the tale is told that kale got its start as a garnish for the buffet line of a famous pizza franchise. Not to eat—just something that looked green and fresh in the midst of all that meat and cheese and bread. (Great marketing, people). I won't name any names, but some people seem to think that curly parsley is meant to be a garnish and only a garnish (they've clearly never tried Jason's grandmother's tabbouleh). Although I generally like to cook or prepare my harvests as real dishes or in salads, I do, in fact, sometimes use harvests for garnishes. When I'm feeling special, I'll put fresh parsley in the bowl of the kids' spaghetti or basil cuttings on their pizza slices. And, would you believe, nine out of ten times, my kids will eat the garnish? (Good for me—"garnish" hasn't been on their vocab tests yet.)

Ferments and Pickles

Fermented and pickled foods are a great way to enjoy that fresh crunch of the garden but keep it around a little longer. Fermenting is all the rage right now and for good reason. Fermented foods have probiotics, which are known to help with immunity and better digestion.

Dry and Dehydrate

Removing the moisture from your vegetables and fruits can deliver delicious garden crunch you can enjoy whatever the weather. Herbs are the simplest and fastest thing to dry. You can simply rinse them after harvest, hang them to dry in a cool and dark spot, and then return to use or store them after they've completely dehydrated.

To dry vegetables or fruit, use a dehydrator or place clean harvests, thinly sliced, in the oven at a low temperature for a long period (we're talking a very long period). You'll want to be certain your harvest completely dries before you jar or store them. But once you do, you'll have a taste of that season sealed away to enjoy when the weather is vastly different (if you can wait that long).

Drinks

Besides eating raw, the second easiest way to enjoy your harvest is to drink it. Tea, smoothies, tisanes—all kinds of fancy things are possible.

Herbs from the garden can be turned into tea simply by cleaning them, pouring boiling water over them, and steeping, straining, and sipping. You can also make tea with dried herbs if you've let them become completely dehydrated. The flavor will be stronger with the latter, but the fresh leaves are still delicious.

Warm Dishes

I'd prefer to be other places besides the kitchen (think about nature!), but I do manage to lift a pot or two in the kitchen every day.

The simplest method I use to prepare my harvest is to broil or roast it. I just use olive oil and sea salt, and maybe some balsamic vinegar every now and again. (I haven't changed a bit since that garden to table brunch.) Cooking vegetables at the right temperature can make a huge difference in the flavor. I cook mine for a short amount of time at a high heat. My methods were confirmed by *Salt, Fat, Acid, Heat*—and now it's official: I'm right.

Get the oven as hot as you'd like it to be, for me that's about 400°F (200°C), cover your veggies with oil and sea salt, place them under the heat source, and cook for a short amount of time (until you get that nice caramelized look). This brings out the natural sugar and I could, honestly, eat the entire tray before my kids get a taste.

Soup

If all else fails, throw your harvest into a soup. Soup, my friend Joyce taught me, is the ultimate superfood because every single nutrient in the food remains in the end product. With other cooking methods, such as boiling, sautéing, etc., some nutrients and aspects of the food are lost to the high heat, the steam, or whatever other chemical process that happens (my husband can explain it). But, with soup, every single last bit of goodness stays in that broth and, if you drink it to the last drop, all that goodness stays with you, too.

Soup is the meal my mom makes for me when I'm on my way home. It's the meal Jason makes on weekends. It's the meal I learned to love when I lived in rural China. Have you heard of "kitchen sink soup" (i.e. everything but the kitchen sink)? Well, I'd like to submit a new, much more appealing recipe (who wants to eat the sink?)—kitchen *garden* soup. Let's make this sound less like a garbage disposal and more like something exquisite, because that's just what it is.

Summary

And now that we've made the soup, it's official: You're a kitchen gardener.

You've got a spot you lovingly refer to as your kitchen garden. And, for certain, you're part of the *Kitchen Garden Revival*. You've changed the landscape of not just your yard but your community and created a new ecosystem for bees and butterflies (and possibly squirrels and rabbits, oops!).

You're growing beautiful and delicious things but, most importantly, you're growing yourself. Each time you tend your garden, you remind yourself that the world is full of unbelievable miracles, that it's okay to slow down, think about nature and fill up on the good stuff. When you're in the garden, you're telling yourself you belong to this moment, to this season. When you're in your kitchen garden you're home. You're making a difference when you share the garden with your family, your neighbors, and when you now look with wonder at the farmer down the road who, somehow, showed up with a hundred pounds of carrots.

Whether you end this book with a pot of chives or a formal potager, you can call yourself "a gardener" who's making a difference, and I couldn't be more proud to call you my friend.

Thank YOU for taking this journey with me, for considering a new way of eating and living and being. Thank you for bringing back the kitchen garden with me. Together, let's think more about nature, fill up on the good stuff, and grow ourselves into who we're meant to be—whole and happy.

Here's to your harvests, big and small, and to making the most of every season. And here's to you—my new friend and partner in this important movement that could literally change the world. Now, please, go share your seeds and overflowing harvests with your neighbor and call me if you ever run out of kale.

All my love, from my kitchen garden to yours.

—Nicole

HOW TO TAKE THE NEXT STEP IN THE KITCHEN GARDEN REVIVAL

Ready to grow your self even more? This revival can't happen without you!

If you've never grown a thing before, don't forget the Gardenary (gardenary.com) step-by-step plan. There are loads of resources in addition to the journal to help you start growing herbs or salad greens right away. Grab yours at gardenary.com/book

Once you've begun to enjoy herbs and greens from containers or small planters, you'll feel the nudge to go bigger. It's time to install a full kitchen garden (even if it's just one raised bed), add trellises or supports, and start growing roots and fruits.

Already growing or can't stop talking about your garden experiences? We'd love to have you on the Gardenary platform as a Kitchen Garden Business or a Gardenary coach. Don't forget: My mission isn't just to bring back the kitchen garden but also to make gardening a viable profession. So, if you've fallen in love with gardening and want to share that passion by coaching and helping others, Gardenary is the place for you. And bonus—you've already completed step one in the application process by reading this book!

As always, share your kitchen garden moments—the wins and the struggles—using #mykitchengardenrevival anywhere you post on the web. I'll be looking for you!

GARDEN LISTING

FORMAL POTAGER

**Spanish Colonial Potager (200 ft²
[18.6 m²]):** Owner: Brian and Resa
Clarke, Designer: Nicole Johnsey Burke,
Featured: 39, 48, 54, 110, 160, 183

**Urban Contemporary Potager (200 ft²
[18.6 m²]):** Owner: Anu Lal & Family,
Designer: Nicole Johnsey Burke,
Featured: 10, 26, 38, 59, 130, 166

FOUR-GARDEN CLASSIC

European Town Garden (64 ft² [6 m²]):
Owner: Cris and Elisa Pye, Designer:
Monica Meyer, Featured: 21, 36

**Uptown Contemporary Garden (128 ft²
[12 m²]):** Owner: Nicolas and Marnie
Medina, Designer: Nicole Johnsey
Burke, Featured: 16, 36, 55, 61, 127, 196

**Southern Creole Classic Garden
(128 ft² [12 m²]):** Owner: Todd and
Amy Mueller, Designer: Nicole Johnsey
Burke, Featured: 25, 36, 152, 175

GARDEN TRIO

**Old World Colonial Trio (175 ft²
[16.3 m²]):** Owner: Andrew and Shanna
Linbeck, Designer: Nicole Johnsey
Burke, Featured: 34, 50, 64

**Modern Farmhouse Trio (90 ft²
[8.4 m²]):** Owner: Jason and Nicole
Burke, Designer: Nicole Johnsey Burke,
Featured: cover, 15, 19, 30, 34, 58, 73, 76,
83, 101, 103, 135, 176, 194

French Provincial Trio (60 ft² [5.6 m²]):
Owner: Robert and Allison Finch,
Designer: Nicole Johnsey Burke,
Featured: 35, 208

TWIN GARDENS

**European Cottage Twin Garden (115 ft²
[10.7 m²]):** Owner: Cary and Julie
Moorhead, Designer: Nicole Johnsey
Burke, Featured: 2, 21, 32, 44, 102, 180

**Spanish Industrial Twin Garden (64 ft²
[6 m²]):** Owner: Charles and Tiffany
Masterson, Designer: Monica Meyer,
Featured: 5, 33, 84, 108

**Formal Traditional Twin Garden (40 ft²
[3.7 m²]):** Owner: David and Danielle
Magdol, Designer: Nicole Johnsey
Burke, Featured: 27, 32, 53, 90

**European Traditional Twin (40 ft²
[3.7 m²]):** Owner: Greg and Nesi
Andrews, Designer: Monica Meyer,
Featured: 21

BORDER GARDEN

**Mid Century Modern Border (90 ft²
[8.4 m²]):** Owner: Ike and Chandos
Epley, Designer: Nicole Johnsey Burke,
Featured: 8, 31, 57, 60, 104

Spanish Modern Border (75 ft² [7 m²]):
Owner: Billy and Christie McCartney,
Designer: Monica Meyer, Featured: 21,
31, 53, 157

**Industrial Terrace Border (30 ft²
[2.8 m²]):** Owner: Julie Pincus,
Designer: Nicole Johnsey Burke,
Featured: 31

**Modern Uptown Border (45 ft²
[4.2 m²]):** Owner: Seth and Rochelle
Bullock, Designer: Monica Meyer,
Featured: 47, 52, 57, 159

**Italianate Border Garden (30 ft²
[2.8 m²]):** Owner: Cary and Amber
Gray, Designer: Monica Meyer,
Featured: 57

CELEBRATE LOCAL

Just in case you missed it in this book, locally sourced materials, inspiration, and help are best when it comes to anything related to food. Here are a few ways to be sure you stay as local as possible.

1. Find local farmers. Look up the farmers' market in your area and go meet the farmers.

2. Join a CSA (community supported agriculture), you'll support a local farmer and learn about your unique seasons and what's possible to grow during them.

3. Visit local nurseries and plant shops. Ask them how they grow their plants and let them know you value naturally and organically grown plants grown by local suppliers. Your vote here makes a huge difference (if you can avoid it, don't shop for plants at the nationwide franchises).

4. Visit and help tend a community garden. Community gardens are a great way to learn all about the local food scene. You'll make instant friends and see how others are already growing in your area. If you're short on space or just want some like-minded friends, community gardens are a great place to hang out.

RESOURCES

Authors on the Local and Slow Food Movement

Wendell Berry

Barbara Kingsolver

Michael Pollan

Forrest Pritchard

Alice Waters

Authors on Kitchen Gardens

Brie Arthur

Mel Bartholomew

Leslie Bennett

Stefani Bittner

Shawna Coronado

Rosalind Creasy

Monty Don

Niki Jabbour

Lauri Kranz

Jennifer Kujawski

Tara Nolan

Ellen Ogden

Maria Rodale and the Rodale Institute

P. Allen Smith

Favorite Cookbooks for Enjoying the Harvest

Any book by Alice Waters

Cooking in Season by Brigit Binns of Williams Sonoma

Farm Cooking School by Ian Knauer

Half Baked Harvest by Tieghan Gerard

Mississippi Vegan by Timothy Pakron

Mostly Plants by Pollan Sisters

Salt, Fat, Acid, Heat by Samin Nosrat

Seasonal Recipes by P. Allen Smith

Simple Green Smoothies and Simple Green Meals by Jen Hansard

Six Seasons by Joshua McFadden

The Blackberry Farm Cookbook: Four Seasons of Great Food and the Good Life by Sam Beall

Vegetables by Martha Stewart

Favorite Seed Companies

Baker Creek Heirloom Seeds

Fed Seeds

High Mowing Organic Seeds

Park Seed

Renee's Garden Seeds

Seeds of Change

Seed Savers Exchange

Southern Exposure Seed Exchange

Territorial Seed Company

Seed Starting Supplies

Johnny's Selected Seeds

Favorite Planting and Tending Tools

Esschert Design: esschertdesign.com

Terrain: shopterrain.com

Sneeboer & Zn

Haws

Williams Sonoma: williams-sonoma.com

Favorite Kitchen Tools and Supplies

Crate and Barrel

Pottery Barn

Target

Williams Sonoma

Nicole's Style Inspirations

Anthropologie

Better Homes & Gardens

First We Eat

Garden and Gun

Gardenista

Magnolia Company

Southern Living

Rifle Paper Co

Wabi-sabi (the concept)

ABOUT THE AUTHOR

Nicole Burke is the Owner and Founder of Gardenary, Inc. and Rooted Garden, Inc. After living overseas and working in the philanthropic field, Nicole wanted to make a difference right where she lived. Once she experienced the magic of growing loads of lettuce in her family's backyard garden, she realized the kitchen garden might just be a thing that could change the world for the better.

In 2015 Nicole founded Rooted Garden (RG) and began designing, installing, and maintaining beautiful kitchen gardens throughout Houston, Texas. RG grew quickly and, as Nicole's online audience grew, her passion to bring back the kitchen garden beyond Houston did, too. So, she started Gardenary in 2017 as an online platform where new gardeners could learn from experienced gardeners through courses, ebooks, classes, and online coaching.

Recognized online by *Better Homes & Gardens* and featured by *Southern Living* magazine, Nicole is crossing her fingers that she's not just growing a company but igniting a movement. By the time her children are grown, Nicole hopes kitchen gardens will be an ordinary thing again and gardening will be a profitable profession for the coming generation everywhere.

Though she comes from a family with horticultural expertise, Nicole is mostly self-taught, and has created her own unique system of kitchen gardening, both in her own backyard and in hundreds of clients' spaces. She teaches the art of gardening with metaphors, satire, and embarrassing stories, aiming to dispel the "green thumb" myth and make growing food accessible and fun for anyone ready to learn. Nicole's message is simple: It's time for a kitchen garden comeback.

Through Gardenary, Nicole has helped thousands of new gardeners perfect their skills and regularly trains hundreds of experienced gardeners to start their own kitchen garden companies. Her dream for the Gardenary platform is that it will provide job opportunities for thousands of experienced gardeners and garden education for millions.

Nicole has lived and gardened in more than five different climates but currently makes her home—and grows her kitchen garden—northwest of Chicago with her husband, Jason, their four children, and their two puppies—Ponyo and Totoro.

Join the Kitchen Garden Revival here:
Online: www.gardenary.com and www.rootedgarden.com
Instagram: @gardenaryco and @rootedgarden
YouTube: www.youtube.com/gardenary
Twitter: @gardenaryco
Tiktok: @gardenary
Podcast: Grow Your Self hosted by Nicole Johnsey Burke

ABOUT THE PHOTOGRAPHER

All of the photos in *Kitchen Garden Revival* were taken with film by Eric Kelley during four photo shoots in 2019 (two in Houston visiting 20 gardens and two in Chicago of Nicole's garden transformation).

Eric was named one of the top photographers in the country by *Harper's Bazaar* and *Martha Stewart Weddings*. He travels internationally to photograph weddings and events and is known for his authentic and delightful imagery. His work has been featured in these magazines: *Martha Stewart Weddings*, *The Knot*, *Southern Living Weddings*, *Style Me Pretty*, and many more.

Eric received a bachelor of arts degree in fine art from the University of Virginia. His goal is to create imagery that stands the test of time in a flawless and personable way.

Eric lives in Charlottesville, Virginia, with his talented wife, Lora, their three children, and two cute dogs.

Learn more about Eric here:

erickelley.com

Instagram: @erickelley

ACKNOWLEDGMENTS

It's impossible to fit all my thanks on one page, but here goes:

Jason: Thank you for being my best friend. I love the life we're growing together.

Carolyn, Brennan, Rebekah, and Elaine: Thank you for putting up with your crazy mom. I love you more than I love my garden (and that's a lot)

Dad and Mom: Turns out you were right about *almost* everything—even the Saturday morning yard work. Your belief in Joannah and me makes everything seem possible.

"Joannah": Not exaggerating to say you're the best big sister a girl could have. Not sure I could make it through life without our chats and texts.

Eric and Lora Kelley: Eric, the biggest THANK YOU for taking thousands of photos to make this book happen—19 gardens in 60 hours and then the epic days in Chicago—only you could make this happen. Lora, the kindest cousin who took my first garden photos, told me to get on Instagram (though I was a doubter), a shining light and one of my dearest friends

Ginger, Elise, and Margaret: Thank you for all your support and for passing the plants with Mom all those years—your examples, each as entrepreneurial women with an artistic touch, have inspired me since I was a baby

Joyce and Bill: Your friendship and encouragement have made all the difference. We love you like family.

The Rooted Garden Team: Monica and Lance, Jill, Jessica, Chris, Chuy, Pedro, Maia, Jen, and so many more. Thank you for joining this wild and crazy mission and making some of the most beautiful gardens in the world.

The Gardenary Team: All the Kitchen Garden Coaches—130 and counting—who have trusted me to mentor you through this process and are bringing the kitchen garden back into your communities, and at www.gardenary.com. The Braid team, Nithya, thank you for making the Gardenary platform launch possible.

Our Rooted Garden Clients: Jenny and Julie who hosted the Rooted Garden to Table Event, clients who welcomed us to photograph their gardens for this book: Resa, Elisa, Shanna, Julie M., Danielle, Tiffany, Julie P., Marnie, Anu, Amy, Christie, Amber, Nesi, Allison. To everyone who's ever paid Rooted Garden a penny to help you grow your kitchen garden: Thank you!

The Gardenary and Rooted Garden online community. You who have hit the "follow" or "subscribe" or the "heart" button. And the thousands of you that have welcomed me onto your screen to teach you more about kitchen gardening, you're the best! Your little taps are changing the world and bringing back the kitchen garden in a way I never dreamed possible. Thank you, friend!

Jessica and the Quarto Team: Thank you for believing in the kitchen garden and taking a chance on me. Creating this book with you has, literally, been a dream come true. May this beautiful book change the world.

INDEX